Praise for
The Very Best Opportunity *for* Women

"This is the best, most well-rounded presentation of this business for the women you'd like to see join your team. It truly captures what makes network marketing so unique."

—UMA OUTKA, EDITOR-IN-CHIEF, *UPLINE JOURNAL*

"Want to know what it takes to be successful in network marketing? Angela and Lisa provide practical advice with tips on how women can maximize their inherent strengths. The women's success stories in this book will give you the boost you need to keep on plugging."

—DEBBIE SELINSKY, SENIOR EDITOR, *SUCCESS MAGAZINE*

"Angela and Lisa have really captured the female soul of network marketing. If you've just joined, or are thinking about joining, the millions of women in this rewarding profession, this book will set you firmly on the path to success."

—RICHARD POE, AUTHOR, *WAVE 3* AND *WAVE 4*

"This book reads with purpose, passion, and pleasure. It's a celebration, of both women themselves and an opportunity worthy of who they truly are."

—JOHN MILTON FOGG, AUTHOR,
THE GREATEST NETWORKER IN THE WORLD,
WWW.GREATESTNETWORKER.COM

"It is refreshing to see a book that truly helps women explore the unlimited possibilities that network marketing offers them. I highly recommend that every woman read this and share it with others in her life."

—PAT DAVIS, AUTHOR, *MIRACLE OF INTENTION,*

AND PRESIDENT, NETWORK MARKETING TUTOR, INC.,

WWW.NETWORKMARKETINGTUTOR.COM

"A must read for every woman who wants to succeed in any home based or network marketing business. Touching, inspiring, enlightening—this book is a treasure chest of experience, and a road map to success."

—DOUG CLOWARD, PRESIDENT,

CLOWARD AND ASSOCIATES CONSULTING SERVICES

The Very Best Opportunity *for* Women

How to Get More Out of Life Through Network Marketing

Angela L. Moore *and* Lisa Stringfellow

PRIMA SOHO

An Imprint of Prima Publishing

3000 Lava Ridge Court · Roseville, California 95661
(800) 632-8676 · www.primalifestyles.com

Information contained in this book has been obtained by authors from sources believed to be reliable. However, because of the possibility of human or mechanical error, or because such information may change after publication of this book, the authors and publisher do not guarantee the accuracy, adequacy, or completeness of such information and are not responsible for any errors or omission caused by the use of such information.

All of the characters in this book are based on real persons, but in some cases, names have been omitted or changed to protect the privacy of the people involved. Therefore, any resemblance to actual persons, living or dead, is purely coincidental, unless authorized by the actual persons mentioned.

All companies and persons mentioned or profiled in this book were selected by the authors solely for the purpose of illustration. All companies are successful and reputable, to the authors' best knowledge, but in no case should the inclusion of any company in this book be interpreted as an endorsement or recommendation by the authors.

PRIMA SOHO and colophon are trademarks of Prima Communications, Inc.

PRIMA PUBLISHING and colophon are trademarks of Prima Communications Inc., registered with the United States Patent and Trademark Office.

All products in this book are trademarks of their respective companies.

Library of Congress Cataloging-in-Publication Data
Moore, Angela L. (Angela Lindauer)
  The very best opportunity for women : how to get more out of life through network marketing / Angela L. Moore, Lisa Stringfellow.
    p.   cm.
  Includes index.
  ISBN 0-7615-2831-8
  1. Multilevel marketing. 2. Women in marketing I. Stringfellow, Lisa II. Title.
  HF5415.126.M663   2001
  658.8'4—dc21   2001021085

01 02 03 04 HH 10 9 8 7 6 5 4 3 2 1
Printed in the United States of America

How to Order
Single copies may be ordered from Prima Publishing, 3000 Lava Ridge Court, Roseville, CA 95661; telephone (800) 632-8676 ext. 4444. Quantity discounts are also available. On your letterhead, include information concerning the intended use of the books and the number of books you wish to purchase.

Visit us online at www.primalifestyles.com

To the great women in network marketing who made this book a reality. And to all of my family, friends, and mentors—especially Lisa, who always add to my joyful role as woman, mother, daughter, sister, aunt, godparent, friend, and single person. I am grateful to all of you.

—*Angela L. Moore*

To Angela who thought I could. To D'Arcy who thought I should. And to Kyle, Maggie, and Ian who liked the idea that Mom was writing a book.

—*Lisa Stringfellow*

Contents _____

Introduction —————————————————

Welcome to Your World!

You are cordially invited to spend some quality time exploring who you are and what it means to be a woman in this new century. Come with us on a journey of self-discovery which we hope will give you some "Ah-ha!" moments as you understand that there truly are differences between various career and life choices.

This book belongs to every woman. Yes, you! It belongs to the woman who is struggling with parts of her life and is looking for a way out, or rather, a way *in* to who she is and what she could be. You could be a mom who wants to spend more time with her family, a mom who wants to stop taking her children to daycare and wants to become the primary care giver for them. You could be a corporate executive who is overworked and underappreciated in the rat race and who is tired of staring at the "glass ceiling" over her head. You could be a single woman who feels lonely because you just can't seem to find a good way to meet and connect with other adults. You *are* a fiercely loyal, intelligent, caring, nurturing person who wants to find her place in the world and, along the way, create a meaningful, passionate, balanced life.

A Celebration of Women

THIS BOOK IS a celebration of women from all walks of life. It is also an introduction for women to understand some choices they can make to achieve a better life status according to their own definition of success. This book is intended to present the new face of network marketing, one that is VERY female.

Over seven million women in the U.S. have chosen network marketing businesses to help them align their passionate purpose, their work, and their life values. Women OWN the network marketing industry: According to the 1999 Direct Selling Growth & Outlook Survey, seventy-three percent of the field sales force are women. By owning a network marketing business, a woman does not have to worry about hitting the glass ceiling, because none exists. Instead, she can find time for her family, enjoy a connection with other women, be surrounded by an atmosphere that fosters relationships, and participate in an industry that provides recognition, appreciation, and promotions based on results.

What You Will Learn

BY READING THIS book, you will learn about relationship marketing and how it allows you to take advantage of skills you already use daily. Your questions about the industry will be answered. In addition, you'll get tips from successful women already enjoying the benefits of owning their own businesses. You will get an objective look across many network marketing companies that offer opportunities to women to enhance their lives. We face the hard questions and present the facts that demystify many mistaken perceptions.

This book is intended to help everyone understand the special relationship and attraction that women and network marketing have for one another. It is a collection of stories about how network marketing has fostered self-esteem and helped change women's lives and the quality of their relationships with their families, mates, friends, peers, and children. Network marketing has provided women with the freedom to make enriching choices and fulfill goals in their lives much deeper than making money. Financial freedom can be achieved through network marketing, but better than that is the achievement of freedom to commit one's life to a higher value system.

Women's Connections to Each Other

IF YOU ARE doing it alone, you're doing it wrong.

The process of putting this book together has burst open the authors' understanding of how women support and provide energy for each other in this world. It was a collaborative effort in the utmost sense of the word, and relationships grew and blossomed along the way. During times of progress, as well as moments of truth, the authors grew as a team who learned from one another, supported one another, laughed and cried with one another. As a result, we each grew in value as human beings and became stronger and better in our friendship, as well as in our connections with others. Our enhanced understanding of what it means to be a woman and how different we are from men has forever changed our perception of the world.

Oprah Winfrey once related that women connect through hardship, whereas men connect through success. While it is obvious that many women join network marketing after moving away from some hardship, the enlightened news is that women in network marketing also celebrate each other's successes and victories. By connecting with the women whose stories you will read and others who contributed to this book, you will learn that great energy can be derived from connection with one another.

In many of our one-on-one conversations and interviews with the women who contributed to the book, great sharing and a special connection on a personal level occurred. In a presentation about the book to almost a thousand women at a seminar, the energy in the room was electric! The positive vibes coming back to support the speakers was overwhelming.

The Female Soul

NETWORK MARKETING GOES deeper than being about money, or status, or things that are produced and sold. It is about being able to help others achieve their dreams. Teamwork is key. This is a characteristic that women display, enjoy being around, and are drawn to. Said another way, teamwork is the essence of the female soul. You are invited to come along with us on this adventure to explore the female soul of network marketing and its connection to a new, more satisfying life for you.

PART ONE

Network Marketing:
The Opportunity for Women

CHAPTER ONE

The Beginning of Your Happy Ending

I T SEEMS SAFE TO SAY that few people want their last thoughts to be, "I wish I had taken more time for my family, friends, and all that I hold dear, and given more of myself to others." If you, like so many women, are already starting to think that way, it's time to reassess where you are and where you want to be. Once you've done that, you can begin mapping a new path to take you where you want to go.

Who Do You Want to Be?

THINK ABOUT YOUR LIFE as it is today. Do you look forward to getting up in the morning; going happily to work; and having plenty of energy to enjoy personal, family, and community activities? Or do you dread your work, longing for time to do what you "really want to do"? Perhaps you identify with Margaret Tanaka, who was backing out of the garage heading off to work one morning when she saw, in the living room window, her newborn baby in the arms of a sitter. They were waving goodbye. "That sight pierced my heart," Margaret remembers. "At that moment, finding a way to get out of the work trap and home to my baby became Goal Number One."

Or are you like Marguerite Sung, who was managing a twelve-person department that calculated take-offs and landings for U.S. Airways? One day, a realtor friend showed her the house of her dreams. "Everything about it was big," Marguerite recalls, "especially the mortgage. But I loved that house and was determined to find a way to buy it."

Or does this story sound familiar? Robin Cohen was in a traditional sales job with a "perfect" salary—high enough to keep her, low enough to trap her. "At that point in my life the concept of earning money month after month for work I'd done long ago was unspeakably appealing," Robin reminisces.

Perhaps you've had similar thoughts and would like to change careers, but you're worried that, if you follow your heart, you won't be able to make a good living. Like many women, you may opt for the regular, predictable paycheck even when it means sacrificing what's truly important to you. There is a saying, "It's better to be about something and get nothing for it than to be about nothing and get something for it." The truth is, it is perfectly possible to be about something—and also make a living at it.

Many women have found a way to do just that by making their work an extension of themselves and their beliefs. Through network marketing and direct selling careers, these women provide products they believe in to their extended network of family, friends, and colleagues, all on schedules that fit into their lives. These women personify the saying, "Do what you love, and the money will follow."

In the September 2000 issue of *O, The Oprah Magazine,* Oprah Winfrey says, "If you want your life to be more rewarding, you have to change the way you think." Maybe now is the time for you to begin reexamining how you think. In this chapter and the next, as we describe network marketing and direct selling, you can evaluate what we say and start to think about whether a career in network marketing is a business path that will reaffirm your values and let you be successful at the same time. Although you may never have considered network marketing—or maybe even have looked down on it—hearing other women's stories of how their lives changed may help you see how this new career might do the same for you.

What Is Network Marketing?

THE TERMS *network marketing* and *direct selling* as discussed in this book are used interchangeably and refer to companies that use independent representatives to market and distribute their products. These contractors—73 percent of them women—engage in person-to-person selling to their network of personal, business, and community contacts. The types of selling in which they engage include:

- Selling to an individual one-on-one
- Selling via a party plan (think Tupperware!), product demonstration, or group selling
- Selling remotely by phone or over the Internet
- Selling directly from a company to an individual brought into the loop by a network marketing distributor

Recommending what they like is natural for women, who do it regularly without pay. As Susan Waitley, now a distributor of USANA nutritional supplements, expresses it: "The most important thing for women to know about network marketing is that you are doing it every day anyway, but just not getting paid. If you go to a good movie, you tell a friend. If you know a good dry cleaner, you tell a friend. Get the picture? Just tell a friend and get paid!"

Many women do not realize the number of personal contacts they make in their everyday lives. These contacts make women valuable recruits for network marketing companies. In return, the companies offer women a solid income and at the same time promote a cooperative spirit and provide opportunities for affiliation, personal development, recognition, and advancement.

Waitley says, "This industry is attractive because most women are caretakers, and network marketing pays us for what we do naturally. It is the only industry where a woman can clear dollar for dollar what a man earns. It's fun!"

Although we know and admire men who succeed in network marketing, we've written this book especially for women—not only because women have innate characteristics that make them likely to succeed in this business, but also because network marketing is a career choice that resolves many of women's employment dilemmas. It is a business that appeals to a woman's heart as well as her head.

Who Is Attracted to Network Marketing?

WOMEN FROM ALL WALKS of life and from every age group are attracted to network marketing and direct selling. Their reasons are as diverse as their backgrounds. You'll hear from women who joined and became successful either on a part- or full-time basis. They include waitresses, housewives, former traditional business owners, teachers, corporate executives, and retirees.

What's the Attraction?

WHAT LURES WOMEN toward direct marketing today? The reasons are as diverse as the lives and pasts of the women who become network marketers. Some women are simply attracted to the "magic" of network marketing. Kerry Lynn Buskirk, independent national sales director for Mary Kay Inc., is one of these. Kerry says the first thing she noticed about Betty Weathermon, her recruiter, was, "She had a sparkle. She was positive and seemed happy. I knew it didn't come from the restaurant where we worked. Betty understood the frustrations we felt working in that atmosphere. The restaurant owners were always more concerned with profits and not their people, who were very loyal, hardworking employees. One day I walked up to Betty, who was the cashier, and said I was getting out of this place, and I was going to sell Tupperware. That was her opening. She told me she was with Mary Kay Inc., and she booked me for an appointment.

"I loved everything I learned about Mary Kay Inc." Kerry is proud that she stayed with her dream and adds, "The Ph.D.'s aren't always the smartest people; they just stay in school longer!" Kerry's suggestion to those considering network marketing is, "I would not take advice from people outside the field who do not understand the marketing plan and have fears about sales. You need to be a bit of a risk taker to do well."

The "sparkle" in Betty Weathermon that Kerry attributed to Betty's association with Mary Kay Inc. is often felt by women who go into network marketing. There are also practical inducements. When asked, women in the business listed these attractions:

- Desire for a career more oriented toward relationships
- Disillusionment with the corporate world
- Desire to learn new skills and develop potential in a new field
- Interest in expanding career and income in a small town with otherwise limited opportunities

More specifically, you'll find that both "push" and "pull" factors account for women's interest and success in network marketing. The push factors are those that make women want to opt out of a business world that is still, at least at its highest levels, dominated by men. The pull factors are those that draw women toward the industry.

Push Factors to Leave a Traditional Job
- Low self-esteem
- Lack of freedom
- Insufficient time for family
- Discrimination
- Unequal pay
- Lack of professional experience

Pull Factors Toward Network Marketing
- Higher self-esteem
- Greater freedom (90 percent work part-time)

- More family time
- More time for yourself
- Greater control over financial security
- Equitable earnings
- Greater recognition
- Opportunity to travel...or not to travel
- Opportunity to utilize and gain skills
- Flexibility

These pull factors make women feel very positive about their careers in network marketing. Women can own their own businesses without the headaches of employees, a back shop to store inventory and process orders, and a large up-front investment. They're also able to link their personal and professional lives and control their own hours so that they have more time for their families, skills training, and leisure activities. Not the least of the pull factors is equitable compensation and the opportunity for financial success, residual income, and promotion. The pull factors are so great that, according to Cheryl Lightle, president and cofounder of Creative Memories, "This growing trend of people embracing network marketing opportunities will continue. I view this as a society searching for the high-touch aspect of personal service in a world that is becoming increasingly technological."

WORK AND RELATIONSHIPS

Women enjoy working in a field where the ability to build and maintain relationships is key and where their informal "credentials"—their talents, skills, and minds—count. One reason for women's success in network marketing—

and their dominance of the industry—is that many enjoy and do well in a field where the business model includes "relationship selling." This is a sales method focused on selling yourself, which in turn enables you to recommend and share products with others and gain loyal customers. Women epitomize this concept. We may not exactly have invented the endorsement method of sharing favorite finds with our friends, but we certainly use it. Whether we're recommending a movie or book we enjoyed, or telling our friends about a new eyeliner that doesn't run or a car that gets great gas mileage, we're effectively selling our ideas and experiences. We also tend to be social engineers, as we fill in the family calendar and volunteer for everything from PTA committees to community projects. In her book, *EVEolution*, Faith Popcorn says, "These institutions that women join are also a vehicle for meeting people, building relationships, finding like-minded people. We all know how women are gifted at finding the common ground, at identifying the ties that bind rather than the differences that divide."

Relationships are at the heart of network marketing. Your contacts (sometimes called your circle of influence) are people with whom you already have good relationships, and now you can share with them both the products about which you are passionate and the opportunity to join you in a financially rewarding business.

There is also the attraction of mentoring. Many women in network marketing become mentors to newer participants, helping them to develop their skills and improve their lives. Often, though, the rewards are more tangible than that. Marguerite Sung of Nu Skin says, "Through network marketing, I have created more than 20 millionaires." What better gift can you offer to your friends?

Lili Willick of Watkins, Inc., which distributes gourmet specialty foods and health products, likens network marketing success to success in waitressing. If you take the time to develop personal relationships with your customers, they'll come back to you—or in waitressing terms, ask to sit in your section.

Work and Family

Another reason women are drawn to network marketing is because this career helps them to balance their lives. It enables you to live in a way that doesn't require that you constantly try to fit your life around your career, but allows you to fit your career into your life. With this balance, you can stop juggling work-family-self and begin living a more integrated life.

Miki Crowl, an Avon representative, is a good example of such balance. She notes, "My two daughters go to different colleges; one plays volleyball and one plays tennis for her school. I am able to make all their meets, yet continue to work wherever I am. I like being my own boss and helping others build self-confidence, as well as their own businesses."

Marguerite Sung agrees: "I can choose when and where to work without getting someone else's approval. Network marketing and women are meant for each other."

This balance can continue long after the family is raised and the traditional career years are over. Teresita Licanan, a recent retiree and Excel representative, says that network marketing "gives me identity, maintains balance in my daily life, and keeps my sanity especially now that I'm retired."

Opportunity for Financial Independence

Financial independence is increasingly a concern for women, many of whom end up being on their own, whether by choice or through death or divorce. For these women, network marketing offers a career that gives them that independence while allowing them to spend significant time with their families. As Miki Crowl expresses it, "I love the freedom network marketing provides, and of course the income. My two daughters are able to attend private colleges and enjoy the luxury of new vehicles."

Self-employment is an attractive option for women who want quality family time, but, done solo without a support group, it can be financially risky. Most businesses fail because of inadequate funding, poor management, computer systems that don't work, or a product line that lacks proven appeal to consumers. Network marketing, where start-up fees are usually reasonable, removes many of the financial risks.

In this industry, women can become entrepreneurs overnight. They can start their own home-based business without needing to create their own product line, develop their own distribution process, hire employees, or purchase an expensive software system to support it. With the proliferation of hundreds of companies in the industry offering a variety of products and services, a woman can, with appropriate research, choose a company that matches her personal interests or passions and is backed by great, proven products and systems. Many network marketing companies have extensive research and development staffs and have invested millions of dollars in computer technology to track order processing, distribution, and compensation plans.

What other industry or business offers the would-be entrepreneur options such as these?

LEARNING NEW SKILLS

The opportunity to learn new skills is another important attraction for many women. Often, direct selling companies offer programs of improvement and self-development that are not only interesting but also lead to higher income. Cheryl Dockery, an independent representative for Primerica (a member of Citigroup), felt the desire to develop skills in new fields.

Cheryl is a college-educated single mom with a teenage daughter. Cheryl, likeable and agreeable, has a sincere desire to help others, and she joined network marketing to help other women become more financially independent.

Cheryl knew that the skills she brought with her would be expanded when she joined Primerica. She would get specialized training, study for and take exams to get licensed, and enhance her recruiting and organizational skills. Her local Dallas group offered almost thirty educational sessions during the summer of 2000, and there were other regional training sessions available to her. Some of the seminars offered included:

- Handling client objections
- Closing a sale
- Understanding the company's compensation plan
- Time management
- Training new recruits
- Goal setting

- Product seminars
- New associate orientation
- Recruiting
- Women in personal financial services

Cheryl's sponsor often says the Primerica opportunity is "The developmental program with a compensation plan attached." This is a great way to describe the valuable developmental aspects of a network marketing organization!

EQUAL OPPORTUNITY

Network marketing also offers women the opportunity to match men in income and position. Although legal and social changes have enabled women to make great strides in recent decades in achieving the same salary, opportunity, and respect as men, some discrimination continues, particularly in the corporate world. The fact is that women frequently are not paid what they are worth.

In network marketing, however, there's no limit to the amount of income or the number of upper level executive positions women can attain, as long as they are willing to meet the requirements. Individuals in network marketing don't win at the expense of someone else, and they can expect to succeed as a result of their merits.

Disillusioned corporate employee Stephanie Stortz, former international environmental engineer and now an independent representative for Excel Communications, was not optimistic when she and her husband entered network marketing.

"When we first began our business," Stephanie reports, "I was not excited to be part of it. My dream was not to own my own business, but to be successful in a corporate setting. I had done everything I was told I needed to do to be successful at my company. I went to a good school and got good grades and then went to grad school and got more good grades. I was busy teaching, working my job, and writing my thesis, and did not have time for one more thing." (Most women will recognize this scenario!) "We started our business because my husband saw the potential—for me! As we built a few things... checks started to appear. And even in the times we weren't working... checks would appear. As I became more and more disillusioned with my corporate situation, I realized that our network marketing business really could be the answer.

"A pivotal moment came eighteen months into our network marketing business when I sat down for my first review with my VP boss at the environmental engineering firm. I was looking for a promotion, but mostly I was looking for the money to go along with all the responsibilities I had taken on. This gentleman was very pleased with my work, but he literally tapped me on the hand and declared, 'My dear, my dear, you'll never make more than $40,000 a year. You're a woman. Your husband's got a great job. What are you concerned about?' About that time, my husband asked me, 'Steph, how much more do you want it to hurt?' I knew he was right—I needed to make some changes.

"I had read a story about a big dog that was lying on a porch. The dog was whimpering and whining and howling now and then. A neighbor walked over from his property and asked the dog's owner, 'Hey, what's the matter with your dog?' The owner replied, 'He's lying on a nail.' The neighbor then asked the owner, 'Well, why doesn't he just get up and move?' The owner replied matter-of-factly, 'It doesn't hurt bad enough yet.'

"That story described my life. It didn't hurt bad enough yet. Well, the hurt had finally arrived, and it motivated me to take action in my network marketing business.

"That fall, I made some choices and some changes. I went back to my job at the engineering firm with a new attitude. I wasn't crabby or tired anymore, but I also wasn't going to work sixty and seventy hours per week anymore, either. I worked my fifty hours, and I took the extra ten hours and built our network marketing business. By Christmas, the part-time income we made exceeded my full-time income at the engineering firm...so I came home. Since that time, network marketing is all I do!"

Betty Miles, now an Excel Communications field leader, is another example of a woman who became disenchanted with her big-profile job. Betty began working on commission for a large insurance company. She discovered first that her male colleagues thought that a "woman's place" in insurance was selling to middle-income teachers and nurses, not to corporations where the big money was. The real eye-opener came when she developed and presented an ideal deferred compensation plan to a company, only to have the sixty-five-year-old bank chairman refer to her as "little lady" and tell her he'd have to meet with her boss before finalizing the deal. She was the boss!

The consequences of this kind of discrimination in the corporate world are almost always financial as well as psychological. Did you ever stop to think, when you read the statistics about the differences between men's and women's earnings, how much money this all adds up to over your lifetime? On average, women working through the 1980s and 1990s who did the same jobs as men earned only 66 percent of what their male colleagues made (the figures ranged from

59 percent to 72 percent over the twenty years). This means that a woman needed to work sixteen months to earn what a man made in a year, or, in a week, work sixty hours to a man's forty to forty-five hours. (As if women have lots of extra time on their hands!) By August, a man in the same job could theoretically stop working and still have earned what it took a woman until the end of December to earn! This is not so in network marketing, where women are paid based on results. Hard work plus great results equals big rewards!

RECOGNITION AND TRAVEL

Women in network marketing can climb the ladder of success at their own pace. As they ascend, they will gain recognition within the industry and the community as solid business people. As they rise in the industry, they can involve themselves at the national level and even broaden their business and personal horizons through travel—should they choose to do so.

Motivated by income and the call of the worldwide planet, Grace Dulaney, presidential director of Big Planet, a company specializing in technology and services for self-owned, home-operated businesses, says, "There couldn't be a better business for the bright and ambitious female who wants the freedom and power to work from home, yet desires to be a part of the big picture of our global economy."

When asked what it was about the business opportunity or products and services that most interested her, Grace responded:

"Two concepts: One is leveraged income. I had just taken my first vacation from my traditional business in four years (people who have their own businesses can relate to this) and went to Australia for a month. Not only did I spend like a fiend while I was there, but my business was closed, so no income came in. This created a 'hiccup' in my income. When I listened to my first Big Planet presentation, the concept of leverage was foreign to me but hit home dramatically. I became painfully aware of the fact that I had no leverage in my life!

"The second concept that interested me was the opportunity in international markets. I had put aside the college dream I had of owning an international business. The trip to Australia resurrected this dream, so I was very open to Nu Skin, the sister company to Big Planet, and the fact that they were at that time just beginning their international expansion. My antennae went up when I heard Australia, Japan, Europe, etc."

Many women like Grace want to move *away* from a traditional business and *toward* network marketing. Many of the stories in the following chapters are of women who came to their network marketing careers because they were trying to get away from unfulfilling work situations. In network marketing they found recognition and the opportunity to broaden their horizons.

Are There Perks?

APPEALING PERKS HAVE always been inherent in home-based businesses. *Red Herring* magazine did a ranking of perks by popularity in the June 2000 issue in an article titled, "Beyond Stock Options." The most appealing perks were casual dress, cited by 82 percent of those polled, flexible hours (60 percent), personal development training (49 percent), and entertainment or company product discounts (40 percent). As a network marketing entrepreneur in charge of your own business, all these perks are available to you!

It's interesting that many of these same perks are now being recognized and implemented by dot-com companies to attract a young workforce. Even some conservative corporations are realizing they need to adopt such policies in order to compete, but such perks are far from standard fare in non-home businesses.

The Language of the Industry

TO INCREASE YOUR UNDERSTANDING of how network marketing works, there are a few words and phrases associated with the business that are helpful to know. The umbrella term for the industry and the selling method used to market directly to consumers on a person-to-person basis (as opposed to a fixed retail store) is *direct selling*. *Network marketing companies* are companies that engage in selling their products through direct-selling methods.

Some terms are interchangeable. For example, individuals who market the products and recruit for network marketing companies are referred to as *distributors, independent representatives, consultants,* or other designations given by the companies. *Network marketers* and *direct sellers* are not employees of the companies they represent. The women whose stories we tell and those whom we quote (other than the corporate executives noted in chapter 6) are all independent business owners and entrepreneurs. We get an idea of how this works from Molly Maxey, an Excel representative who is from a small town that offers few career opportunities. "There are approximately forty-five executive senior directors in Excel," Molly explains. "Among these are my husband and me, my son Jeff Cates, and (on my fourth level)

Shane Douglas. We have three of the executive senior directors out of over one million representatives that have come through Excel! We all come from very small towns in northern Idaho. We threw out a challenge to each other to see who could get promoted first. Even though we started our businesses at different times, we were promoted to the highest position in Excel one day apart. Shane is in the Top Forty earners, my husband and I are in the Top Sixty, and Jeff is in the Top One Hundred. Not bad for a group of people who had no prior networking experience!

"Our original perception about multilevel marketing was that it was all about pestering friends and family into buying things they didn't need so the salespeople and the company could make money. If I had known in the beginning that Excel was network marketing, I never would have gone into it. After joining, I realized that I didn't have to get people to do anything differently. They were already using the phone; now they would just be using my service.

"I can do the things most people only dream about. Each day is mine, not my employer's. And I don't have a business that owns me; I own it. I believe network marketing gives women the opportunity to be on the same playing field as other professionals. No matter what their abilities are, women can use network marketing to achieve the same financial goals as others with better skills and education."

MULTILEVEL MARKETING

The next term in our glossary, *multilevel marketing,* is sometimes used interchangeably with network marketing, but it more correctly describes the payment plan, not the approach to selling. In the past, traditional direct selling companies generally had single-level plans that paid representatives commissions for each sale. Later, some companies created residual income and added override components to their plan. This allowed distributors to earn from sales made by the distributors' recruits, or made by others recruited by someone they sponsored. The collective group on which a distributor gets paid overrides is known as a distributor's *organization, genealogy,* or *downline.* Downline refers to those you recruited directly or indirectly, who now have business units under you, or are "down the line" from you in the organizational hierarchy. *Upline,* on the other hand, refers to those who are "up the line" or above you in the organization hierarchy. Currently in use by many companies is a multilevel compensation plan, a blend of sales commissions and organizational overrides known as a *hybrid compensation plan.* These plans reward activities having to do with sales, recruiting, leadership, and retention (keeping people, rather than allowing turnover of the sales forces). The different compensation plans are discussed at length in chapter 3.

The Final Test: Is Network Marketing for You?

HERE ARE SOME QUESTIONS you may want to ask yourself about your current situation, based on what we have said so far. If you decided to invest an additional eight to ten hours a week, do you think your boss would allow you to work a flexible schedule that would let you earn what you are worth during that time? Should you overcome that hurdle (which in itself is doubtful), would your boss agree to any of the following?

- Pay you residual income over and over for your initial efforts?
- Allow you to choose with whom you work?
- Allow you to do something you are passionate about?
- Allow you to have a mentor who wants you to succeed and get promoted?
- Allow you to be a mentor to others?
- Allow you to go to great conventions?
- Allow you to go to workshops to develop your skills?
- Give you recognition when you deserve it?
- Enable you to be connected to a great community of people with whom you can create lasting relationships?
- Allow you to and still earn money while your Web site keeps selling your products?
- Let you create your own dress code?
- Allow you to deduct expenses associated with your job?

If your employer offers all these benefits, and you love working where you are, by all means keep the job you have! On the other hand, if you wish your job offered some or all of these benefits, consider the network marketing alternative. Nancy Jo Ryan, independent consultant for The Pampered Chef, is one who's glad she did. She tells us this: "When my daughter was six and a half and my son was almost a year, I wanted to look for a job that would give me some Christmas money. It was the beginning of September, and my criteria for this job was as follows: I didn't want to work weekends, I only wanted to work two nights a week, I had a commitment on Wednesday nights, and I wanted the month of December off! In fact, I probably was only going to do whatever job I found for two months and quit. I had to make at least ten dollars an hour with no child-care costs. When my husband said, 'Oh, your boss is going to love you,' I realized I was looking for something very specialized. I truly wanted it all. That's when I began looking into direct sales companies. A friend told me about The Pampered Chef. I made the call to a consultant and started my business two weeks later."

Overcoming the Fear

MOVING INTO WHAT may be uncharted territory isn't easy. Carol Totten, now a representative for Excel Communications, remembers how reluctant she was to take that first step. "My sponsor bugged me for three months before I ever took a look at the business," she recalls. "When I finally did, I signed up immediately."

By now, because you know something about what network marketing is, you may feel more comfortable taking your first step in exploring this career choice. You may, for example, see things differently, as did Margaret Tanaka, a Shaklee representative, who tells us, "When I began to see sales as a service to others, all my fears dropped away."

You, too, may begin to appreciate why network marketing is the very best opportunity for many women. As you continue through this book, your familiarity and appreciation will grow; as you venture forward, you can consider if you just want to be smart, or if you will become brave enough to take the steps that will enhance your life.

As Suze Orman, a financial consultant, says in her book, *The Courage to Be Rich: Creating a Life of Material and Spiritual Abundance*, "If you can start to change the thoughts that say you can't into thoughts that say you can, you can begin to change your financial destiny."

CHAPTER TWO

Network Marketing's Female Soul

As WE HAVE SAID throughout chapter 1, we firmly believe that network marketing offers a great way for women to uphold their values and make significant money at the same time. Certainly, the over seven million women in the United States who have chosen to join network marketing companies know and understand that there is something unique going on between network marketing and women! We have thought hard about this and have come up with a possible reason. It's what we call the "female soul" of network marketing.

What Is a Business with a Female Soul?

ACCORDING TO *Webster's Tenth Collegiate Dictionary*, "soul" is the "animating principle or actuating cause of an individual life," or "the quality that arouses emotion and sentiment." By adding to this definition the qualities associated with women—their ability to nurture, to show appreciation, and to build supportive relationships with others—we arrive at what we call the "female soul." In our minds, a business that uses, fosters, and exemplifies these qualities is a business in which women flourish—it is a business with a female soul. Because network marketing, in all its aspects, is so essentially about nurturing people and building relationships, we view it as having this female soul and as being the industry where women not only can be themselves emotionally and psychologically but also can enjoy significant monetary success.

When women in network marketing were asked what they are most proud of in their network marketing businesses, they said:

The women I work with. They are so wonderful. They are my best friends and we've all grown so much together.

—MARGARET TANAKA, SHAKLEE CORPORATION

This company has given me the opportunity to make a difference in many women's lives.

—CAROLYN A. WARD, MARY KAY INC.

The loving relationships that have developed over the past four years. The real people whose lives I've helped change.

—CAROL TOTTEN, EXCEL COMMUNICATIONS

Being able to have a positive influence on my team members' personal growth and success.

—LILI WILLICK, WATKINS INC.

The lives I've seen change.

—BETTY MILES, EXCEL COMMUNICATIONS

In this chapter we will explore how different the female soul in network marketing is from women's experiences in corporate life. We will also share stories of nurturing and relationships that occur often in the network marketing environment. First, let's look at what happens in corporations.

Rules of the Corporate Game–
The Myth Dispelled

DO A GOOD JOB and follow the rules of the game, and you will be justly rewarded. This is the myth of corporate America. The trouble is, the rules are often difficult to identify. Even when you closely follow what you think the rules are, and you have a set of objectives to reach and you "deliver," rewards are often elusive. Does the corporation guarantee that you will get the raise you deserve? Or is it possible that raises have been capped by a corporate salary survey, or that management dictated a maximum of 5 percent, when you deserve 10 percent or more? Do bonus plans that sounded good at first shrink over time? Is the bar to advancement raised so high that you don't even try making the jump? How can anyone win in this unpredictable situation?

Every day, deserving employees—both men and women—are overlooked for promotions. Many don't even know why, because generally no explanation is offered. Have you been surprised to see people get promoted even though their work was clearly mediocre, while a deserving worker is bypassed? Do you sometimes wonder whether a promotion was political? Or whether the boss promoted a personal favorite for reasons unrelated to the worker's ability? If the "loser" was a woman, was the position "above the glass ceiling?" And if the "loser" was a man, did he somehow fail to match the male model of success in a corporation? These all-too-typical occurrences leave many corporate employees feeling that their bosses don't appreciate their value, which in turn leaves employees with a feeling of helplessness, of being out of control. Whatever I do, you might feel, will not be enough. Even if you work hard, are loyal, and do an outstanding job, you still may not get the reward you deserve. And to further undermine the work of most women, "appropriate" payback appears to be about 15 percent below that of their male counterparts. Such diminishing of their relative value leaves many women doubting their worth and experiencing lower self-esteem. How sad—especially when we all need positive feedback. Contrast this corporate situation with the experience of Carolyn Ward, independent national sales director of Mary Kay Inc. Carolyn says, "The business opportunity offered me the opportunity to earn what I was worth—not what the job was worth." Corporations have a long way to go to balance and integrate both male and female characteristics if they hope to attract the best talent!

Network Marketing's Female Soul

COOPERATION, NOT COMPETITION among organization members, is the practice in network marketing. Let's take a look at some of the foundations and guiding principles of the industry, which respond to and offer fulfillment for the actuating cause of our "female" side, what we are calling the "female soul." The female soul seeks to express its instinctive desires to nurture, cooperate, give everyone equal opportunity to win, to help, to create a passionate purpose and be justly rewarded and recognized for contributions. Network marketing reinforces all these values.

Values Alignment

The values encompassed in network marketing align with women's inner core and instinctive desires because they:

- Embrace the Golden Rule
- Involve nurturing, mentoring, and helping others
- Follow "rules of the game" that are clear and fair
- Offer recognition and appreciation that are expressed
- Allow room for everyone to succeed
- Provide a venue for self-development
- Offer opportunity to connect to a community
- Foster meeting new people and provide singles with the opportunity to be social
- Allow women to put their natural assets to work

Diane Grunseich likes her career in network marketing because her Excel Communications business allows her "to raise money for organizations that need funds to do whatever needs to be done to make goals and dreams a reality." Diane does fund-raising for the Special Olympics, a women's shelter, the high school marching band, and the Red Cross. She says, "The world needs compassion, and I hope that I am doing my very best to help those who are in my path. People helping people is really what the world is all about."

Margaret Tanaka of Shaklee is another network marketer with a desire to make a difference in the lives of others. "I liked my job in public television production," Margaret explains. "The reason I got into it was to be part of quality programming that would make a difference in the lives of others. I was hoping to make documentaries but those opportunities didn't come up. After six years, I realized that I felt isolated. I wanted to work more closely with people. I decided I needed to find a career that was more relationship-oriented, and it was critical to me that my work reflected my values. I had to know that I was making a difference in the lives of others. I went on a retreat to think about this career transition, and that's where I heard about Shaklee for the first time.

"Now I'm able to stay home and be with my son when he's not at school. I travel around the country and give leadership seminars. I really enjoy it. I am in complete control of my schedule. I love it! I volunteer with my free time—and am currently working on developing a food program in Haiti. I visited Haiti in January and will return in July. I can take off as much time as I want from my business to help people. I never would have had the time, income, or freedom to do this in a traditional job."

Grace Dulaney of Big Planet expresses her career satisfaction in poetic language: "My mission is to enrich lives with abundant gifts of passion, awareness, and divinely inspired grace. Big Planet is my palette from which to paint, my stage on which to dance . . . it provides the vehicle in which I can fully express my purpose."

Working Within Your Values, Not Against Them

If you're working for someone else, work probably takes a huge chunk of your waking hours—not only the 40-plus for which you're paid, but the hours you spend on commuting; getting dressed; purchasing, washing, and ironing; and picking up your dry cleaning. Many women dread going to work and live for weekends and vacations. Work for them is a chore, not the labor of love it could be. By defining what's important in your life and being determined to honor your priorities, you too can achieve your own simply abundant life!

Valeria J. Bagnol, independent national sales director of Mary Kay Inc., found that network marketing with its female soul enabled her to define and meet her priorities. "My initial intention was to make some extra money for grocery shopping," Bagnol tells us. "I grew to like it because I was enjoying what I was doing. I started making much more than grocery money. Now I am able to take better care of the self, holistically. Because I enjoy what I am doing and am more financially stable, my mind and my body are more relaxed. I take more vacations, worship more, and am able to purchase more of the things that make life more enjoyable. I was able to pay out of pocket for my son's college tuition, which I would not have been able to do otherwise."

Room for Everyone

Network marketing provides an environment where everyone involved can succeed and better his or her status and does not do so at the expense of colleagues. Network marketing typically has an unlimited number of "higher-level" positions, which creates a female-friendly, win-win scenario. The organization chart is often described by the terms we mentioned in chapter 1. It may be called one's "genealogy" (a very woman-friendly, family tree image), downline, or simply one's organization. Although it may look like a hierarchy on the surface, it allows everyone to progress without excluding anyone.

In the male model of a corporate structure, only one person at a time moves up while others are held back. Two best friends may find themselves competing for a position that only one can get, thus changing their friendship dramatically. In network marketing, it is possible for everyone at the same level to be promoted at the same time, and no one needs to be left out. Instead of competing with peers or best friends to go for that one open position, a person who meets the requirements will get a raise, and often many people are promoted together. When anyone gets promoted, everyone can celebrate! Individuals who don't receive promotions know they didn't fail because somebody else succeeded. They know full well that they control their own destinies and can achieve the next level by setting personal goals and meeting clearly specified requirements.

Indeed, your promotion is in the best interest of your superiors in rank. It will often result at least in your superiors receiving larger bonus checks and can in fact mean that they will get promoted, too. The traditional female characteristics of cooperation, nurturing and helping others to do better are the very spirit of network marketing. What a different environment is created when everyone is motivated to help everyone else succeed!

Mentoring People vs. Managing People

The spirit of cooperation doesn't stop when you become a manager of your own organization, as is possible in corporations where new managers may find it hard to work up their own motivation or inspire others to go the extra mile. That's because corporate workers are typically expected to do what's needed so the corporation can meet goals and timelines that may not match their own. Even when you can get a staff member to take on an unappealing project and accept a ridiculous deadline (possibly via coercion!) you probably haven't the authority to reward the employee tangibly; you just have to hope that an end-of-the-year performance review will result in appropriate compensation.

As Stephanie Stortz says, "One of the biggest things I didn't like about my job was that I wasn't necessarily helping anyone. If I helped others in my office, my boss thought I wasn't busy enough and gave me extra projects. With my network marketing business I get paid to help others! I love that concept! The more I help others achieve what they want, the more I get what I want."

In Business for Yourself, but Not by Yourself

Network marketing commonly creates a tight-knit group and a support system that fosters success, growth, and emotional bonds among members. Women network marketers are business owners in business for themselves, but not by themselves. Kerry Lynn Buskirk, the former waitress who now has her own Mary Kay business, says, "I was in a beauty salon recently, and the owner, who worked by herself, mentioned to me that although she knows a lot of other women in her field, she did not feel there was a support system. There was no one she could go to for advice on a regular basis or when she needed a little pumping up. I think a lot of women who are in business feel that way. They love the independence, but it can be lonely. The down times are discouraging. I have never felt that way in this business, because of our support system."

In network marketing, you are in business for yourself, but you're also working with other women in the same profession. You can reach out to motivate others. You aren't butting heads with the people you have recruited for your organization or struggling to figure out how to make a corporate goal meaningful to this or that individual. Rather, you're helping that person to achieve her own goals. This lets you act more as a mentor and a helper. Instead of pushing people to respond, you can use rewards to pull them toward an action, for which they'll be tangibly rewarded under the company's career and compensation or recognition plan.

The "you-do, you-get" philosophy kicks in as a great motivational benefit. The payback, too, is much more immediate (weekly, monthly, or quarterly) than is an annual raise.

FEMALE-FRIENDLY DUTIES OF A NETWORK MARKETER

A good network marketer, of course, needs "the right stuff." Let's take a look at the specific duties and qualities one needs to succeed and how a woman's natural talents can play a role in her success. The basic responsibilities of an independent representative for a network marketing company are:

- Finding customers, generally by using warm market contacts (see page 43 for explanation)
- Finding hosts for parties or workshops if it is a party-plan business
- Demonstrating, sharing the benefits of, and/or recommending products or services
- Recruiting others who want to participate in the business opportunity
- Training, leading, and acting as a mentor so that others may succeed
- Motivating others and recognizing their accomplishments

Because women in general are blessed with the gifts of being good communicators and networkers, they tend to perform these tasks well. As Molly Maxey, an Excel representative, says, "I was gifted with a big mouth. I used to be condemned for it, and now I get paid for it!" We have discussed the innate qualities attributed to women: the desire to nurture and develop others, the urge to recommend and share finds with others, and the ability to lead a group cooperatively. The fact that they possess these characteristics attracts women to network marketing—and network marketing to women.

GET PAID FOR WHAT YOU DO, NOT FOR WHO YOU ARE

The nice part of network marketing companies compared to regular corporate jobs is that network marketing fosters a you-do, you-get strategy. This makes network marketing a great leveler of people. What you must do to succeed—levels, promotions, status, bonus incentives, and contests—is spelled out. When you accomplish the goal to which you aspire, you are rewarded accordingly.

Network marketing companies' compensation plans offer equal opportunity for everyone. Payout is not determined by one's background, education level, sex, ethnicity, or personality. Nobody gets ahead simply because the boss likes her. An individual's accomplishments are acknowledged and rewarded; whether or not she is liked or disliked by someone higher up is irrelevant. And whoever you are, once you achieve results, you get specified rewards. Sometimes it is the quiet reward of an increase in your paycheck because two more customers are buying your product. Or it may be very public recognition, as when you walk on stage in front of 5,000 people at a convention to get your pin or ring for achieving a designated level.

It's possible for a network marketer to find herself earning more money than the boss who held her back at her previous corporate job. Participants can even pass their "upline" without any negative consequences. This win-win aspect definitely has its roots in the female characteristics of the business.

RECOGNITION AND APPRECIATION

Women—quite rightly—often feel that their hard work in a traditional job goes unnoticed or is taken for granted. It's not unusual for women to come up with ideas or achieve goals only to have their male bosses or coworkers take credit for them—or undermine their value. This is sometimes an "honest mistake," resulting from the inability of many men—and sometimes women—to recognize that women are capable of significant contributions. At other times, these people are undermining the "competition" so they can "get ahead" in the game.

People, however, need acknowledgment and rewards for their work, and the network marketing environment is particularly conducive to providing that recognition. Recognition can be the primary factor that cements women, who traditionally are less likely than men to receive workplace recognition, to a company. If corporate America recognized its workers as well as network marketing does, corporate America might indeed attract more women. This relative shortfall in recognition and effort may explain why many corporate "opter-outers," both male and female, often turn to network marketing.

Recognition need not be a monetary reward. According to an article in *InStyle Magazine,* after rehearsal for the Academy Awards show it is a tradition for each of the presenters and performers to receive a gift of goodies in a Longaberger (a direct selling company!) hand-woven basket. "Everyone likes to get a gift," says Michael B. Seligman, executive producer of the 2000 Academy Awards. "Because these people receive no compensation, we give them a gift basket as a special thank you."

All human beings like to hear other people say, "Yes, you exist; you matter." In the book, *Paychecks of the Heart*, Mary Kay tells the story of a hostess, we'll call her Patty, a woman who always wore clothes that were "too short, too tight, too revealing" and the doubts that Kerry Buskirk had in inviting her to a hostesses' awards meeting in a small Kansas town. Kerry lived by the Mary Kay saying, "We should never prejudge based on outward appearances" and invited Patty, who brought her mother as her guest. Patty came dressed conservatively that time, but her mother had very long gray hair and wore overalls! Patty won the award as "top hostess" of the month. Kerry watched "as tears streamed down the mother's face when her daughter's name was called, and her scruffy appearance melted into that of a smiling and proud mom."

Several months later, Patty called Kerry to say that her mother had died. Overcome with emotion, Patty went on to tell Kerry, "At your meeting, when I was recognized as top hostess, it was a very special occasion for my mother. No one in my family has ever done much of anything besides get in trouble. I have two brothers in prison, and you probably know I work as an exotic dancer . . . That evening was the first and only time in my mom's entire life that she ever had any reason to be proud of any of her kids. She told me it was the proudest night of her life, and she was happy to know that I might find a better way of life by associating with nice people like you."

When these kinds of things happen, you realize you're not only building a business, you're restoring a soul.

Such a simple thing, yet recognition is a key component of the success of network marketing companies. This simple courtesy of acknowledging other individuals' self-worth reinforces that they have meaning. And it's this meaning that motivates people to do well and to achieve satisfaction in life.

The Missing Link and Essence of the Female Soul

IN A WAY, it is sad that people crave recognition from network marketing companies, because this reflects what little acknowledgment they get in other areas of their lives. Women often do not feel appreciated for the contributions they make on their "regular" job, and they are sometimes even taken for granted even though they are loved by their own family, spouse, or children. It's great to be part of an industry that so richly offers the feminine spirit programs of recognition to fill this wide, wide gap. Carolyn Ward of Mary Kay Inc. says about network marketing, "We practice the Golden Rule: 'Do unto others as you would have them do unto you.' We understand women and their needs. We know what it takes to be a strong leader. I plan retreats, guest events, and meetings, which the women in my organization support. There is tremendous bonding at these events."

The Golden Rule is a good way to sum up the strengths of network marketing. The female soul of this business truly promotes and fosters an environment in which everyone can join hands in the spirit of helpfulness and cross the finish line in victory together! If this appeals to you, network marketing may have a place in your future.

CHAPTER THREE

The Past and Present of Network Marketing

N ETWORK MARKETING has a long and rich past as a marketing and distribution method. Throughout its history, it has relied on person-to-person contacts, personal testimonials, endorsements of products or services (sort of a QVC up close and personal), and the involvement of people with goals and dreams bigger than their current circumstances afforded. Network marketing offers a business opportunity for those who want to become involved.

Because people are so much the heart and soul of this business, as our individual and collective lifestyles have changed, so has the business. The industry is continually reinventing itself to offer contemporary products, technology supports, and enhanced opportunities that allow people to improve their lives.

To fully understand the opportunity network marketing presents for you, knowing something of its history can be helpful. How did it begin? When and in what ways did women become involved? Let's take a look.

A Brief History of the Industry

MORE THAN 100 years ago when network marketing started, the companies who pioneered non-store retailing primarily did direct selling door-to-door. This concept dates back to the Avon Lady, who went from house to house wearing white gloves and a hat, and the Watkins man, who drove his horse-drawn carriage through neighborhoods selling his liniments, extracts, salves, and such. (As we well know, Avon cosmetics remain popular to this day. The J. R. Watkins Medical Company, which manufactured and distributed various home remedies in 1868, continues to thrive today—as Watkins Quality Products, selling nutritional and health products made of fresh botanical and other natural ingredients.) Back then, it was easy to use the direct selling approach, as most middle class women stayed at home, retail stores were hard to get to, and selling took place right in the home during the day. Only a handful of companies existed then. (Poor women always worked: They had no choice.)

It was in the 1970s and 1980s that women began a mass migration from the home to the workplace. The dream seemed to be to attain equal opportunity with men. Women gave over their measurement of worth to corporations whom they imagined would validate their talents by recognizing their contributions and promoting them within the ranks.

While working outside the home seemed to be the answer to women's prayers in those decades, many individuals developed negative feelings as a result of their corporate experiences. Layoffs, firings, lack of promotion, the realization that working hard and doing a good job were not necessarily rewarded, and the amount of time away from family and loved ones (especially for working mothers) all deflated women's expectations. A new, more woman-friendly dream arose, that of working from home and achieving financial independence.

In response to this desire, network marketing businesses experienced a growth spurt. They offered individuals a chance to create something of their own and to work toward financial freedom. This allowed women to be with their children and offered the practical tax advantage of keeping more of what they earned, by incorporating their businesses into their daily lives.

WOMEN'S ROLES IN THE HISTORY OF THE INDUSTRY

Even in the early days of direct selling, women pioneers in the industry were forging relationships and helping each other succeed. Some of this is captured in *The Oral History of Direct Selling* put together by the Direct Selling Education Foundation (DSEF). Since then, few stories capture the female entrepreneurial spirit as do the stories of Mary Kay Ash, who founded Mary Kay Cosmetics, and Mary Crowley, the founder of Home Interiors. The fascinating relationship of these two phenomenal women is described in *Direct Selling in the United States: A Commentary & Oral History* by Morris L. Mayer. In the excerpt below (reprinted by permission of the DSEF) Mary Kay recalls her early influence on Mary Crowley:

> I am the one who introduced Mary Crowley to direct sales. Mary impressed me. Her personality was so terrific. She was the secretary to the president of a furniture manufac-

turing company. I said to her, "Mary, with a personality like yours, why in the world are you behind a desk? You would be great in sales. How much do you make?" Of course that was none of my business, and she looked at me with a look that concurred that it was not; but she finally said, "I make sixty-six dollars a week." I told her that I did, too, on bad weeks. That impressed her.

We both had three children, and I told her I was home [for them after school]. At that time, we had no freeways in Dallas so the problem of getting home in the afternoon traffic was terrible. From downtown, you were just in a slow, no-movement line. That always made her unhappy because she didn't get home until 6:30 or 7:00 and she was never there when her children got home from school. So I impressed her with the fact that I was there because I left my Stanley [Home Products] party at 4:00 and I beat that traffic business from wherever I was and so I got home in time to see my kids come in from school. So I said, "If you are ever interested, I'll offer you a job as a Stanley dealer."

About a month later she called me and said her husband, David, was going on three months' active duty with the National Guard. She wondered if that might be a good time to try out the Stanley offer on a part-time basis. At that time, if you worked part-time, you'd only make eight or nine dollars tops for a night's work. If you weren't going to hold ten parties a week, there was not really much use in my fooling with you. But I told her that while I didn't think it was worthwhile for me to even teach her to do the job, she had such a great personality that I would say yes and try it. So I took her to a Stanley party the very next night.

After about three months, she called me up and said she was going to be at the sales meeting on Monday. She had never been to a meeting, and I said, "Good heavens! Did I make a mistake? Is it a holiday or something?" And she said there was no mistake, but she had resigned from her secretarial job and Monday was the first day she'd be available to go full-time with Stanley.

Sometime later, Mary left Stanley and joined World Gift. To make a long story short, I went to a World Gift show with her and I was intrigued because she was having such fun. When I saw all the glamorous gift items from India, England, France, and all over the world, and they were so pretty and the people were so enthused, I thought, "Gee, this is wonderful." So she recruited me!

I joined World Gift in 1952 and left on May 13, 1963. Mary Crowley, in the meantime, had left World Gift and started her own company, Home Interiors & Gifts, about two years earlier. I started Mary Kay Cosmetics on September 13, 1963, on a Friday—Friday the thirteenth. I was very, very unhappy with the way women were being treated. I had met many women who I thought were smart, capable, but did not have any opportunity. In the early sixties, women just didn't have a chance in the corporate world. I did get on the board of World Gift, but I might as well not have been there. Every time I suggested something, they would say, "Mary Kay, you're thinking like a woman again." Well, our sales force was 100 percent women, and they should have listened, but they didn't. And that was one of the things that really did get to me. So I started thinking about what I could do to overcome some of the problems I had encountered.

This, of course, is not the end of the Mary Kay and Mary Crowley stories. In fact, it just tells us about the beginnings of what were to become two companies—Mary Kay Inc. and Home Interiors, which joined Avon and other pioneer direct selling companies to become the foundations of this growing industry for women.

NETWORK MARKETING TODAY

Let's fast-forward to the year 2005. It's hard to imagine the door-to-door scenario in today's environment where consumers are seldom at home during the day, shopping malls are everywhere, and Internet shopping fills the computer screen. Network marketing companies have moved from the door-to-door model to what is termed the "sphere-of-influence" model. While network marketers still use their everyday contacts as the basis for starting a home-based business, today's model is based on the principle that companies bring good products and systems to distributors who in turn bring customers to buy the products. They also bring potential distributor contacts who are part of their circle of influence and are known in the business as the "warm market." This is the secret formula, and it is the envy of all consumer marketing and e-commerce companies.

Because direct marketing appeals to so many, for so many reasons, women are turning to this opportunity and finding unprecedented success. Women finally dominate— perhaps even "own"—an industry. According to the Growth and Outlook Survey conducted by the Direct Selling Association (DSA), women run 73 percent of all network marketing home-based businesses. We believe that there's a good reason for this. Although men also succeed in the industry, women have a special advantage because they are, many psychologists believe, natural networkers and nurturers who place more emphasis than do men on relationships and affiliations with other people. The good thing is that women can make money at the same time they are leading fulfilling business lives.

How Earnings Work: Compensation Plans

AN IMPORTANT INGREDIENT in network marketing today is the compensation plan or plans that a direct selling company offers to its representatives. It goes without saying that the more effort you put into a direct selling career, the more likely it is that you will earn a good income. Companies feature a variety of packages to reward their independent contractors. Here's a quick overview of the four basic kinds now in use.

STAIR STEP/BREAKAWAY

In the profitable but complex stair step compensation plan, you "climb the stairs" by selling more products and bringing more sellers into your genealogy or organization within the company. The higher you climb, the bigger your bonuses get and the more bonuses you have access to. The "breakaway" part refers to those whom you have sponsored, who then "break away" from your organization after they too have climbed the stairs to a certain level.

These are among the most profitable plans available because there's no limit to how wide (frontline people whom you have personally enrolled) or how deep (large organizations underneath you) you can build. (A *wide organization* has one person who has personally sponsored lots of frontline people. A *deep organization* is one in which the lines are made up of lots of people who are actually recruiting others into the organization, who in turn form a new lower level.) Because payout is greater for those with larger organizations (as your business matures, you'll be earning more), those who benefit most from it must be comfortable waiting for their rewards.

UNILEVEL PLAN

The unilevel compensation plan is one of the simplest plans to understand. It sets a limit on the number of levels from which you can draw commissions, but no limit on width.

MATRIX PLAN

The matrix compensation plan limits frontline responsibilities but not growth. It is similar to the unilevel plan except that it limits the number of distributors on the first level. Recruits brought in after the maximum number of first-level positions has been reached are automatically placed in other downline positions.

BINARY PLAN

In the binary compensation plan you are paid for depth, but growth must be managed. You build two "legs," a right leg and a left leg, each of which consists of distributors you recruit and train (or who are recruited and trained by someone under you). In most cases you are paid commissions only on the sales total of your weakest leg (the good news is that you are paid for the volume of the entire leg!). This compensation structure provides incentive to keep your "legs" producing equal or nearly equal sales. To be well rewarded, you need to constantly manage the sales and recruiting of your two legs.

Demystifying the Industry: The Straight Scoop on the Pyramid Question

ONE QUESTION OFTEN comes up when you share a network marketing opportunity with someone unfamiliar with this legitimate industry that generates $23 billion in retail sales volume in the United States alone. You may be asked, "Is it one of those pyramid schemes?" It's amazing how this undeserved lumping of large, legitimate companies with a small number of unscrupulous perpetrators of pyramid schemes continues to prevail. It's like assuming that all major reputable retail stores are engaged in illegal practices if a couple of clerks cheat on giving change. It's just not fair. Still, you will need to become comfortable in answering the question, which at some point will surely come up.

"Pyramid scheme" is a technical legal term signifying a fraudulent system of making money from an endless stream of new recruits. Let's take a look at it in simple, lay terms. Legitimate network marketing companies pay commissions and bonuses on the movement of products or services to consumers. In contrast, a pyramid scheme pays out money to people already in the plan from fees or monies paid by new people coming in. In essence, new recruits give money to their recruiters, then enlist their own recruits who in turn give them money. Often these are called "head-hunting" or recruiting fees. The amounts can be exorbitant. Sometimes, instead of a fee, the new recruit is required to purchase a huge amount of inventory, without the ability to move it to the ultimate consumer. If new recruits stop coming into the business, no fees are collected, inventory loading stops, and there is no new funding to pay off the other participants. Eventually, the "pyramid" collapses.

The pyramid question came up in a political context for Betty Miles of Excel when she wanted to start in network marketing. Betty explains, "My new husband was the Secretary of State of South Carolina. It was a reelection year, so he wasn't crazy about the idea of his wife doing this type of business. He thought his opponent would use it against him. He thoroughly checked my company out before agreeing to let me try it, but he asked me to only recruit people he didn't know. He didn't want me talking to our neighbors, church members, political supporters, or friends. I ended up asking a lot of insurance people and a bunch of Democrats (my husband is a Republican)."

Betty went on to earn a million dollars and become a member of Excel's Million-Dollar Masters Group. The governor of South Carolina introduced her as "the biggest little capitalist in South Carolina."

One easily understood but unlikely example that can help you get the gist of and better understand what a potential pyramid scheme consists of is the Social Security system in the United States. Past contributors such as retirees and disabled former workers actually get their checks funded by existing workers and new workers coming into the plan who make payments to the plan's fund. This money is not held for each individual's future funding needs, but it's paid to former participants. If the workforce shrinks and less money is put into the plan while the number of retirees increases, there is a threat of the plan collapsing due to lack of funds. If new members don't continue to come into the plan to provide a source of funds, then no payments can be made. This is what happens if a network marketing company structures its compensation plan illegally.

While there have been and still are a few scam artists in network marketing, most legitimate businesses can be recognized because they fund their compensation plans by selling their products. This means that, even if recruiting stops, as long as the product is sold, commissions can be paid. A review of chapter 5, Choosing a Company, will help you identify reputable companies and avoid the pyramid scheme pitfall.

Industry Self-Regulation–
The Spirit of Cooperation Continues

ONE MEANS OF making sure you're dealing with a legitimate network marketing company is to check with the industry's national organization. Most reputable companies in the industry belong to the Direct Selling Association (DSA), a self-policing organization in Washington, D.C. Member companies cooperate with one another and conduct important initiatives to keep the industry viable. There is a collective presence on Capitol Hill and individual lobbying efforts with members of the U.S. Congress. There are joint efforts globally through an international council, which works to keep direct selling opportunities open around the world. The educational arm, the Direct Selling Educational Foundation, offers consumer education programs and conducts on-campus days at participating universities. The industry also keeps and provides statistics on sales growth, number of companies, types of products sold, and other useful information. To maintain the integrity of the industry, all member companies agree to operate under a strict code of ethics.

The New Definition of Success

DIRECT SELLING IS a serious industry dedicated to helping its members succeed at whatever level they choose to participate. Success is not always about money. Many women who have thought about their career aspirations have decided that, for them, a simple, balanced, and joyful life is the definition of success. Their direct sales careers give them these intangibles as well as a good income. Duncan Maxwell Anderson, the editor of *Network Marketing Lifestyles,* understands this when he writes, "Women are smart. They'd rather learn how to have a good life than figure out how to cope with a bad one." He observes that the way to depict a woman who has it all is no longer a woman who's got "a hectic, high-level job at some corporation; a hectic, successful husband; a hectic, fabulous house; and two hectic kids in day care somewhere." Rather, it's a woman who has a life, who can stay home with the kids if she so chooses, perhaps homeschool them, and go on vacations. He says of women in network marketing, "These women know very well what's first, second, third, and last in importance."

Llewellyn J. Rhoe, a male Excel representative who was formerly a trainer for Men Are from Mars, Women Are from Venus, shares Anderson's perspective from a man's point of view: "I'm a man. My wife likes me. Actually, I'm deeply in love with Helene (my wife), so the fact that we can be together all the time is the real draw here. As soul mates and the love of each other's life, [network marketing] is the best of all possible worlds. This is the only way we could have a true life together, pursue our passions, and grow old together! Our goal is to master the art of living together."

Many people engaged in network marketing have made similar comments about their experiences. Network marketing is an industry offering financial success and emotional fulfillment. We've discussed the past and present—now the future is up to you!

CHAPTER FOUR

Network Marketing Income

A Different Way to Earn Money

I MAGINE HAVING YOUR husband tell you that he'd join your business as soon as your *monthly* income equaled his *annual* income. Marguerite Sung's corporate-lawyer husband did. And Marguerite Sung's Nu Skin *income* did just that. Today the ambitious pair works together.

Imagine finding a business so profitable that it not only paid your current expenses, it helped you pay off past business debts too. Lili Willick did. Her seemingly successful traditional business of building management and janitorial services left her in debt. Today the profits from her network marketing business have helped her work her way out of and well beyond those debts.

After Margaret Tanaka's husband died, she knew she'd need time to grieve. So she gathered her group and told them that for a while she'd be flying at the back of the pack; they'd have to lead themselves. During Margaret's almost one-year break, through the loyalty and dedication of her group, her income not only held steady, it rose.

Susan Waitley was passionately building her organization when a brilliant idea came to her: Why not make my kids a part of my business? So she enrolled each of her seven kids into her organization. Today those children are earning from $400 a month up to $1,800 a week. "They always loved me," Susan says. "Now they *really* love me!"

These examples illustrate some of the factors that distinguish network marketing income. In this chapter we'll take a close look at these and other advantages that set this income apart from other ways of earning money. In the first half of the chapter we'll review the elements that make a network marketing income distinct. In the second half, we'll give you two insiders' views of how compensation plans work and how to proceed if you're getting started.

Network marketing has some earning advantages that you may or may not be able to find in the corporate world: equitable income, unlimited income, and more "affordable" income. But the principal way that network marketing income is distinct from the income you'd earn at an office job is that it offers multiple streams of income.

"When I started this business I didn't understand the opportunity. All I knew was that I loved the products and I enjoyed telling others about them," Susan Waitley says. "Incredibly, that was enough to be successful in this business. Had I known a bit more, I would have been even more successful."

No Limits

WANT A QUICK WAY to test your financial IQ? Put a 20-dollar bill on the desk in front of you. What are you most likely to do with it? Call for a pizza and rent a movie? Give in to that cotton tee in the season's newest color? Or sock it away at 6% compounded interest as you save your way toward your million-dollar retirement fund?

You've done the math and you can deny it no longer: To make ends meet you need an extra $300 a month. What's your plan? Sever all spending? Call your local paper and ask about delivering papers at 4:00 in the morning for $10 an hour? Or, find a way to do what you're already doing, but start earning money for it?

Contrary to popular opinion, the key to financial health is not simply getting a larger income. Nurturing your relationship with money—paying attention to it, understanding it, and never diminishing its worth—will have a much more profound effect on your financial health than simply acquiring more of it.

EQUITABLE INCOME

Government statistics tell us that in 1999 a woman earned approximately 75 cents for every dollar that a man earned. But in network marketing a woman earns one dollar for every dollar that a man earns. In essence, then, network marketing offers a woman a 33 percent pay raise over other industries.

This issue of equal pay for equal work will resonate more strongly if you have had first-hand experience with this so-called gender wage gap. "One of the many reasons I love this business is that it pays women and men equally," says Marguerite Sung. "I had been managing a department for several years when I hired a new male employee to work in my department. Though he worked for me and was brand new to the company, my boss felt he should have a salary bigger than mine. It was a hard reality to live with."

"When I worked in corporations I had to convince my boss of my worth," says Watkins Distributor Karen Hagen. "In network marketing, I'm demonstrating what I'm worth. While the corporate world 'thought' I was worth only $20,000, the world of network marketing knows I'm worth ten times that!"

RESPONSIVE INCOME

Suppose you wanted a raise, had worked harder than you'd ever worked before, and made a measurable difference in the department. Are you sure you'd be rewarded for it? And do you think the reward would match your effort? Most companies give you only one chance each year to get a raise. And very often they limit those raises to some predetermined percentage.

In network marketing, if you have a bang-up month, you get a bang-up check the next month. In other words, the income you earn is highly responsive. Create results, and you'll get a raise. You don't have to wait. You don't have to hope your review falls on a day when things are going well for your boss.

UNLIMITED INCOME

A network marketing organizational chart looks like a web, a tree, or a mountain range. No one person stands at the top. Rather, lots of people are standing on lots of peaks throughout an organization. A corporation, in contrast, really has only one person at the top.

Inside a corporation, your salary is essentially capped by the size of your boss's salary. It doesn't matter what you do, or what you make happen, you won't earn more than your boss. And if your work warrants a promotion, again, your salary probably will be capped by your boss's salary. How many times have you felt in your working life that your contribution equaled or exceeded that of your boss? Did your salary reflect that? In network marketing if you have what it takes to move rapidly to the top, your income will rise with you. It doesn't matter what your upline earns. Many, many new distributors quickly surpass their sponsors. And at no point will your income potential max out. Keep achieving, and keep increasing your income.

MORE AFFORDABLE INCOME

What we do with our money can amplify the dollar or diminish it. To understand your true earnings, you have to look beyond salary and consider all the other costs and savings that an opportunity will encompass. For example, suppose you were offered two jobs, each of which paid $25,000 a year. These jobs might *seem* to offer the same financial rewards, but if you look at them closely, you'll see that they don't. One may require you to work slightly longer hours or have a lengthy commute. One job may require a formal business wardrobe; the other may permit casual attire.

Network marketing is often considered a more affordable way to earn a living because your costs can be lower and your benefits greater. Let's look at an example (figure 4-1) to see specifically how a corporate salary might compare with a network marketing business.

Your comparison chart is likely to look different. The point is to help you build your own chart. A still more sophisticated comparison chart might also include the time costs and tax benefits. Also, the earnings for a network marketing

Network Marketing's Affordable Income

	Traditional Employment	Independent Network Marketing Distributorship
Income	$30,000/yr. or $2,500/mo.	$12,000/yr. or $1,000/mo.
Hours Worked/Month	160 hours/month	60 hours/month
Daycare Costs: Assuming you have only one 3-year-old child.	$700/month	$200 (Even with a home-based business you'll still need daycare.)
Commuting Costs: Assuming you live 15 miles from your corporate job and that your driving costs are 30 cents per mile.	$180/month	None
Clothes: This of course depends entirely upon the individual.	$250/month	$100
House Cleaning: $40 twice a month.	$80	0
Restaurant Lunches:	3 times/week @ $6/lunch, or $72/month	0
Eating Convenience Foods:	$75/month	0
Net Earnings per Hour: Income minus expenses divided by hours worked per month	**$1143 net earnings @ 160 hours per month = $7.14 per hour**	**$700 net earnings @ 60 hours per month = $11.66 per hour**

Figure 4-1

business are representative of a new business rather than a mature business. Over time, your earnings could be substantially higher than $12,000 per year.

The surprise in this particular example is that even if your corporate salary is more than twice what your network marketing earnings are, you still could be earning more per hour by having a home-based network marketing business. Also, if you're earning $30,000 a year, you probably imagine that your net hourly earnings are greater than $7.14 per hour.

TAX ADVANTAGES

The tax advantages are hard to estimate, as they would vary from individual to individual, but their impact on your net income could be substantial.

If you're a rookie money manager, you're likely to focus on your gross income (your total earnings) when you think of how much you've earned. A more mindful money manager knows that it's net income (what you keep after taxes) that's the more relevant number.

Here's a small sampling of the kinds of items that may be considered business expenses and therefore deductible: advertising costs, start-up costs, part of your mortgage, part of your utility bill, auto expenses, some of your dry cleaning costs, food costs if you serve food during your presentations, travel costs if you do some business while traveling.

MULTIPLE STREAMS OF INCOME

We all know it makes sense to diversify our investments. But do we understand how important it is to diversify our incomes? This is what multiple streams of income are about: Finding simple and creative ways to create more than one source of income.

In network marketing you can create multiple streams of income simply by telling someone from your circle of influence about the business that gives you the freedom and flexibility you want in your life. Each time your suggestion generates a business builder who then tells others about the business, you have created a new stream of income.

> I'VE OWNED restaurants; clothing stores; a chocolate factory; apartment buildings; commercial buildings; seminar companies; newsletter businesses; and direct-mail, multimedia, and software businesses. I've invested in Broadway plays. I've even owned a piece of a professional basketball team, the Utah Jazz. Network marketing beats them all.
>
> —Robert G. Allen, author of
> *Multiple Streams of Income:
> How to Generate a Lifetime
> of Unlimited Wealth*

RESIDUAL INCOME

Inventors, authors, and songwriters all earn residual income. And so do network marketers. Residual income is money that comes in month after month for work you did months, even years ago. It's a flow of money that is not dependent on today's effort. And it's one of the most exciting benefits of network marketing.

"The night the concept of residual income was explained to me, I couldn't sleep," says Oxyfresh Distributor Robin Cohen. "In fact, I had trouble sleeping for many nights after I first understood residual income. You see, at the time I was selling seafood—about $7 to $8 million worth a year. But if I took even one day off, my income was affected. With that moment of understanding residual income, I knew my life would chart a different course."

Think of it this way: Have you ever planted a bunch of daffodils into the cold fall ground; then watched them bloom prodigiously in the spring? The next year there are even more daffodils and so on until finally after putting in just a few dozen bulbs, you have a huge area of "naturalized" bulbs?

Like those bulbs, a network marketing business also tends to naturalize. You can talk to one person who talks to many more people and before you know it, you have a strong organization simply from speaking to that one person.

And if you have a network marketing business, you never know just who you might enroll. When Susan Waitley was in Australia helping USANA start its Australian business, the hotel's housekeeper asked Susan about her business. With Susan as her coach, today that woman is a top distributor of USANA, creating yet another stream of income for Susan.

> WHEN I speak to adults who want to earn more money, I always recommend the same thing. I suggest they take a second job that will teach them a second skill. Often I recommend joining a network marketing company.
>
> —Robert Kiyosaki, author of *Rich Dad, Poor Dad*

Understanding Your Compensation Plan

YOUR FIRST EXPOSURE to a network marketing compensation plan is likely to strike fear in your heart. What does it all mean? Can I be successful if I don't understand the compensation plan? Can I begin talking to others before I fully comprehend the compensation plan? Are there tricks that an insider understands that I don't yet know?

INTERVIEW WITH A COMPENSATION PLAN EXPERT

Doug Cloward is widely regarded throughout the industry as the resident expert in developing network marketing compensation plans. In his twenty-five-year network marketing/direct sales career, Doug has created many compensation plans for many different kinds of network marketing companies. He not only understands them; he knows what makes them work and what makes them fail. In the following interview, Doug shares his insights into network marketing compensation plans.

Q: *Suppose I'm just getting started, and I don't really understand the compensation plan. Can I start building my business even though my understanding is weak?*

DC: Absolutely! Your success in this business depends on your ability to network, *not* on your ability to understand the compensation plan. Start by understanding just the first aspects of the plan, your retail commission, for example. To motivate yourself toward growth, look ahead and see what you'll need to do to advance to the next level.

Q: *What should I focus on in the beginning?*

DC: You want to start by building a solid customer base. When you do this, the others you bring into the business will mimic you. When each distributor has a solid customer base, you have a healthy organization.

Q: *Is there one core concept that drives a compensation plan?*

DC: Yes, creating sustainable volume is really what it's all about. You have to have products that deliver real value to real customers who are likely to come back again and again. You have to set performance levels that are both sufficiently attainable yet somewhat of a stretch. When you build from a core of sustainable volume, you have a plan that works.

Q: *It's tempting to think that those who are doing really well in this business are doing something special. Are they?*

DC: Yes, they are working this business on a consistent basis. The successful distributors work their businesses virtually every single day. They're talking to lots of people. But do they have some kind of secret weapon? No, it's just a matter of getting out there and talking to people.

Q: *What's more important to my success, finding products that I enjoy selling or finding the best all-around compensation plan?*

DC: Though both will be important to your success, the most important element in your success is to find products that you enjoy telling others about. If you find that, a good compensation plan will amplify your efforts.

Q: *Can you explain the idea of building wide and deep? And which is more important to do?*

DC: When you have a wide organization you have many people underneath you whom you have personally enrolled. When you have a deep organization you have personally enrolled others who have personally enrolled others and you then have a deep (many layered) organization.

Generally speaking, width determines profitability and depth determines stability. If you had limited time resources and had to choose between building wide or deep, you should opt for building wide.

Q: *Which is more important to my success, customers or business builders?*

DC: Both will contribute to your success. The idea is to look for customers with your antennae up for potential business builders. Without a solid base of customers, no business will succeed. Customers generate retail commissions. Business builders generate residual income. As your organization grows, the bulk of your income will shift from largely retail commissions to largely residual bonuses.

Q: *What about the minimum monthly requirements? How are they set?*

DC: They're very important to the health of your business. If they're set too low you won't have the volume you need to be profitable. If they're set too high, people can't achieve them and they'll drop out. There's usually a "sweet spot" that's between $200 and $500 per business builder per month. This gives you the volume your business needs without having to establish unattainable monthly requirements.

Q: *Why do retail commissions vary so much from company to company?*

DC: Retail commissions for big-ticket items are likely to be lower than commissions for lower priced products. If the average order size is $500, your commission percentage is probably going to be smaller. But if your average order size is around $50, you're likely to have a higher percentage commission.

Q: *Is there a point in time when the selling part of your business stops and your role as a leader to your downline becomes your entire focus?*

DC: A compensation plan will reward you for doing four different activities: selling, recruiting, training, and leading. In the beginning stages of your business you will be doing more selling than leading. And as your business more fully matures, you'll be doing more leading than selling. To sustain your business through its inevitable highs and lows, however, you'll want to make sure that you're spending at least 25 percent of your time selling product. Remember: What the leaders do, the others in the organization mimic. And customer sales/sustainable volume will always be the foundation of any successful business.

Remember This: This Is a Business!

TALK TO LILI WILLICK about her business, and you quickly realize that this is a woman who understands money. Her work as a bookkeeper, office manager, and now successful Watkins distributor sharpened her awareness and understanding of the financial aspects of this business. Here's her financial advice to the new network marketer:

When my husband and I started our Watkins business, we decided to simply do as much as we could for three months and take it from there. If we were to start again today, we would have had a much more specific business plan. Every business, regardless of how modest or massive your goals are, should begin with a business plan. At the very minimum a business plan should include the following items.

A statement of your goals. What are you hoping to achieve? Create a vacation fund? Equal your current income? Or build a significant source of asset income? And what kind of timing are you expecting?

A specific step-by-step plan for reaching those goals. Decide what kind of income you're after and then work backward to create a month-by-month plan for achieving your goals.

Designated times in the week that you'll devote to achieving your goals. Once you have these assigned times, be sure to use them wisely. Although a first-class filing system and catchy flyers can have their place, if you want to see income fast, get out and make contacts! Talk to people. Prospect continuously.

Agreement among family partners regarding your plan. Let your family members see their benefit in your business plan. Show them what hours you'll be working your business. Tell them what you're hoping to accomplish. Their support will smooth the path toward your goals. And when dinner's an hour late, they'll know why.

There are lots of tax benefits to having a home-based business. So I'd suggest that everyone—even part-timers—should speak to an accountant to help them take full advantage of the tax implications of having a home-based business. Be sure to look for one who has experience helping people from the network marketing industry.

You can write off a portion of your mortgage and your utilities as a business expense if you're working from your home. Also, you can contract your kids to work for you so that their salary (what used to be called their "allowance") is now a business expense. Then they can use their salary to buy their school supplies so that money that used to be fully taxed is now a business expense.

Reduce your accountant costs by keeping good business records. You can set up a simple filing system and then with just a few minutes each week you can keep it up-to-date. You should have records showing what you invested in your business each month, how much you sold, how much you spent on buying products for your own personal consumption, and an automobile log. (My accountant suggested keeping a small notebook in my car and each time I made a business trip I just made notes about who, what, when, where, and why I had used my car for business purposes.)

The other thing an accountant can do is help you work smart. For example, my accountant will notice if I'm spending a disproportionate amount on advertising or promotions, or if I'm not spending enough on those kinds of things. When members of my organization ask when they should quit their day job, I advise them to proceed very, very cautiously. If you move too soon, you can expose yourself to some stress if things don't go exactly according to the plan. You don't want to operate your network marketing business—or any other business—in this mode. It may take more sacrifice to continue with your job and build your business, but it will be less stressful. See if you can cut back on your hours. In my particular business I estimate that it will take two to five years to fully replace your current full-time income. If you want to take the leap and can afford to, just remember this isn't a holiday. You want to build this business with your goals and your work schedule clearly mapped out.

I also advise that you have fun! The more fun you're having the more people you'll attract to yourself and your business!

Where you take your network marketing business is up to you. Make no mistake: this is not easy money. But when your talent, passion, and commitment are strong, you can accomplish more than you ever thought possible.

CHAPTER FIVE

Choosing a Company

The Key to Freedom, Flexibility, and Fulfillment

ONE OF THE quickest ways to gain a lot of knowledge about living well is to read the small book, *Life's Little Instruction Book*. Among the nuggets of wisdom that its author, Jackson Brown, Jr., offers is this gem: "Choose your life's mate carefully. From this one decision will come 90 percent of your happiness or misery." What's good advice in marriage is also good advice in network marketing. Choosing your parent company is the most important decision you'll make should you decide to try network marketing. Select carefully, and you'll speed your cycle of success and experience its rewards for a lifetime. Choose poorly, and you'll experience frustration—if not failure—in your efforts to build a network marketing business.

This chapter, which is designed to help you understand the pieces that fit together to form a good decision, includes four sections:

Finding Out What Matters Most to You
Knowing What to Look For
Knowing What to Look *Out* For
The 25 Most Important Questions to Ask Your Finalist Companies

Our goal is to give you a comprehensive guide for choosing a lifelong business partner. Readers won't find all the issues we discuss equally important—each individual will read with different questions in mind. Customize your approach to fit your interests, talents, values, and goals. Combine the guidelines in this chapter with your personal road map, and you'll be on your way to finding a company that defines success as you do and also offers what you need to succeed in the years ahead.

You'll discover *products* you're passionate about. You'll locate a company with *values* that you share. You'll find a *selling system* that works for you. You'll meet a *sponsor* who will simplify and enhance each and every day that you work. And you'll track down a *compensation plan* that rewards you as you'd like to be rewarded. So do your homework now and reap the benefits for a lifetime.

Unfortunately, not everyone who goes into network marketing does the research first. Some people leap before they look. They may do well anyway, but their success will be less certain than if they'd investigated the possibilities before choosing. Your colleagues who didn't take the time to research the parent company won't have such a broad understanding of the enterprise or of how it compares to others. Keep in mind that the homework you do now will be tremendously valuable to you from the minute you begin your business. Due diligence before you sign a consultant agreement will put you ahead of the game. Not only will you be making a wise personal choice, you'll also have lots of credibility as you recruit others into the business. Your knowledge will give you enormous credibility with those you talk to about joining your business. Choosing well is the first and most important step you'll take toward success in network marketing.

Section I: Finding Out What Matters Most to You

WHAT ARE YOUR OBJECTIVES? A little extra money? Total financial freedom? Tax benefits? What are your needs? More meaningful work? A home-based business? A business you can build among friends? Balance between your personal and professional life? Travel? Recognition? A combination of these? What are your passions? Nutrition? Cooking? Home decorating? Skin care or cosmetics? Technology?

WRITE OUT YOUR OBJECTIVES

Pull out a sharp pencil and a piece of paper. (Make that a gorgeous piece of paper, worthy of valuable planning!) Write at the top: Here's What I Hope to Achieve Through Network Marketing. Start writing and keep writing until you have uncovered all of your deepest motivations. What is that restless voice inside you saying? What would make you happiest? How much time can you realistically commit to this business? Let all those thoughts flow out.

By doing this exercise, you'll be better able to make a wise and well-considered choice. These thoughts will also help you target your efforts once you start your business.

To further identify your goals, create a wish list. Cut pictures from magazines showing what you hope to achieve: perhaps a new car, a new house, more confidence, financial freedom, a business built from home. Visualizing your goals in actual pictures will help make them real. Pretend that anything's possible. What would your "anything" be?

Once you know what you want, look for companies that offer you the opportunity to realize your goals. If, for example, your motives are financial, zero in on the economics. If you plan to reach high, find a compensation plan that rewards its top earners heavily. If you can only commit to part-time work, but finances are still key, find a compensation plan that offers good payback to its smaller sellers. Or figure out just how much effort you'll have to put in to earn $500 per month—or $5,000 a month if that's your goal. It may also be important for you to favor companies that offer consumable products and typically cater to repeat customers.

WHEN Margaret Tanaka first encountered Shaklee's environmentally sensitive household products, she saw the light: Everyone who uses them becomes part of the solution rather than part of the problem. "I'm not selling Basic-H when I tell others about Shaklee, I'm serving the Planet."

Maybe your motives aren't entirely financial. Perhaps work that's emotionally or intellectually meaningful is a larger objective. If that's the case, look closely at the character of the company and the kinds of products or services it sells. Learn all you can about the person who's running the company. What are his or her values? Find out what charitable organizations the company supports. Ask about the "good works" the company performs. What about the products? Are they changing lives or just keeping cars shiny? Or if they are keeping cars shiny, are they using environmentally friendly products to do so? Down the road these things will matter to you—a lot!

Still another big reason for building a network marketing business is the opportunity to work among friends, make new friends, and expand your social life. If this is your goal, attend company meetings and make sure that this company markets to people with whom you have something in common. Also put some energy into finding a company supervisor who shares your values and can inspire you to greater heights. The point is to zero in on what's key to you.

Understand the Investment You're About to Make

One of the big selling points about having a network marketing business is the low start-up cost. Consider this: Start-up costs for a GNC franchise (General Nutrition Center) range from $112,000 to $197,000. Start-up costs for a Jenny Craig Weight Loss franchise range from $150,000 to $314,000. But you could start a network marketing company, with a full line of well-regarded, highly competitive nutritional products or a comprehensive, state-of-the-art weight-loss program for less than $100.

Lili Willick, a 12-year Watkins distributor, and her husband, Wendell, labored for years trying to build traditional businesses. Although they looked successful—big contracts and lots of clients—their expenses were greater than their revenues. "After owning traditional businesses, the Watkins opportunity looked very good," says Lili.

The Watkins line of spices was immediately appealing. But she didn't grasp the opportunity until she'd attended a company meeting. "Here I saw things from a business person's perspective. Products that people are already buying. Products that they buy over and over again. I'd simply be asking my customers to switch from the stores to me. And once they switched, they'd return again and again."

It's wonderful to be able to begin a business of one's own for such a small amount of money. Still, you need to understand that in network marketing, your real investment isn't as much money as it is time and effort. So instead of racing forward because the start-up fee is so reasonable, think of the time and effort you're about to invest and make sure that you're doing it with the right company.

One final note before you get started: Time teaches us that the best decisions are made when we listen to our hearts, brains, and souls. Our brains identify smart choices, our hearts gravitate toward joyful choices, and our souls will validate wise choices. So pack up the many parts of your being and go make a brilliant choice.

Section II: Knowing What to Look For

BELIEVE IT OR NOT, in this business nothing trumps passion. Pure, heartfelt passion outperforms—in terms of worldly success—knowledge, experience, business savvy, connections, and clout. So the first and most important thing you can do is to find a company with products you can be passionate about.

FIND PRODUCTS THAT EXCITE YOU

If a product doesn't "find you" first, the Direct Selling Association (DSA) might lead you to products you can be excited about. As they will tell you on their Web site (www.dsa.org), "The DSA is the national trade association of the leading firms that manufacture and distribute goods and services sold directly to consumers. The association's mission is "to protect, serve and promote the effectiveness of member companies and the independent business people they represent." In other words, the DSA is a good resource for well-regarded direct sales or network marketing organizations. Their Web site also has links to member company Web sites, so you can do a lot of basic research in a relatively short period of time. Log on and learn about the companies that interest you.

The DSA Web site also provides company descriptions and key facts about the more than 150 members of the Direct Selling Association. Just go to the "member company" section to learn more about which companies sell (among many other things) jewelry, nutritional products, skin-care products, cookware, long-distance service, home care, parenting products, art, cosmetics, toys, water treatment, weight management plans, and even wine! And keep in mind these are only the companies that are actual members of the DSA.

Remember, your initial goal is to find products that interest you. Do you enjoy preparing creative meals for your family? Do you have a much-loved drawer full of cosmetics and skin-care products? Have the Internet and emerging technologies caught your attention at its highest level? Do you believe in the saying "you are what you eat"? Would you wear a T-shirt that said "So Many Books, So Little Time?" Do you reduce, reuse, and recycle? The point is to think about yourself and the kinds of things you're inclined to be passionate about and then find companies offering products that match your interests.

Before you make your choice, "date" a few of the companies first. Order products, look at their literature, call their customer service department and ask questions such as these:

- What's your product guarantee?
- Where was your company's last convention held?
- What's your top-selling product?
- Who are some of your top distributors? Would you ask them to contact me?

The more you probe, the more you'll know.

Then, once you've narrowed your options, do some serious research. Begin with a list of three or four companies. Contact each one and ask them to send you some company literature. Once you get it, read it. A few pieces of paper can carry lots of messages via words, pictures, statistics—even through the quality of paper! You can get a good sense of the following:

Who is the company?

What are they saying about themselves?

How would you feel sharing this literature with others?

Do the product claims feel substantiated, or are they somewhat outlandish such as "effortless" and "rapid weight loss"?

Does the company present a positive quality image?

What's their mission?

What kinds of people do they feature in their catalogs?

Remember, once you become a distributor, that literature will become a central part of your business. Make sure you connect with it.

Warm Spirit Consultant, Sandy Christensen certainly did. She states: "When I first saw the Warm Spirit catalog sitting on the seat of a friend's car, I had to learn more about the company. It was the most beautiful product catalog I had ever seen. I became a distributor in large part because of the beauty of that catalog!"

Many network marketing companies either have their own research and product development facility or are connected to one. This can be a tremendous resource for distributors. The Forrest C. Shaklee Research Center, for example, has a staff of over 60 nutritionists, biochemists, dietitians, and more, working solely on product quality. USANA, founded by a nationally known scientist, Myron Wentz, Ph.D., is also known for its sizeable commitment to research and development.

FIND PRODUCTS THAT EXCITE OTHERS

Your first hurdle is finding products that *you feel passionate about.* Your second hurdle is finding products that *others will appreciate, too.* Generally, what your customers will insist on having is a product that satisfies a need or desire, is well priced, and offers some advantage over the retail marketplace (very often, that advantage is you!).

A lot of the network-marketing corporations have been built on the concept of everyday products that we need to replace constantly—nutritional supplements, soaps, detergent, and the like. In other words, these companies have chosen something for which the need has been established and is constant, so that customers will return again and again. Companies like Shaklee, Excel, Avon, Watkins, USANA, Melaleuca, Cell Tech, Mary Kay, and Nu Skin have done this with products such as shampoos, nutritional supplements, cosmetics, spices, telecommunication services, weight-loss products, and more.

And although selling consumable products is a tried and true way to achieve success in network marketing, it is by no means the *only* way. The Longaberger Company, which sells one-of-a-kind handcrafted baskets, is close to being a $1 billion company. And The Pampered Chef, which sells kitchenware, has annual sales in excess of $600 million. The products behind these success stories aren't consumables.

Make sure that the product that captures your interest is also competitively priced. Compare both the retail and network marketing alternatives. Keep in mind that many network-marketing products are unique, and you probably will not find a true competitive alternative. Melaleuca, for example, was years ahead of the retail marketplace when it tapped into the Melaleuca Oil's vast properties. This is an antifungal, soothing oil product with a lot of unique selling points.

Next, does the product offer uniqueness—something that the retail market can't deliver? This may be the most important hurdle of all. Even if the product you're selling is something your prospective customers use each and every day, you will still be asking them to do something they don't normally do: buy from you rather than at a store. In other words, you must somehow be able to show people how your product somehow differs from what's already out there. Very often your offering is unique because your customers are purchasing it from a knowledgeable salesperson who has personal experience with the product. Just be sure you know what distinguishes your product from others and that you're easily able to talk about it.

FIND A COMPENSATION PLAN THAT WORKS FOR YOU

An entire book could be written on how to understand and evaluate compensation plans. For every expert who professes that his or her plan is the best in the industry, you can find a counter-expert who can argue with equal conviction for another plan. When a plan shines brightly in a certain area, it can't afford to be equally strong in others. That is, when a company returns all the profits to its distributors, programs for those distributors—customer service, conventions, recognition, product training, and more—will undoubtedly suffer. Keep in mind, too, that some companies have gone under because they offered compensation plans that were *so* good, *so* rich, and *so* rewarding that the company simply could not survive.

The next question to ask is what compensation plan the company uses. You're most likely to hear about these four types:

- Stair Step/Breakaway: Profitable but Complex
- Unilevel Plan: Comprehensible but Limiting
- Matrix Plan: Limits Frontline Responsibilities But Also Limits Growth
- Binary Plan: Paid for Depth but Growth Must Be Managed

(For a quick overview of the four basic kinds of compensation plans, refer to chapter 3.)

People who build homes for a living often tell their clients that while there are three variables in the construction business—quality, size, and cost—the client can only choose two of the three. Similar limits apply to network marketing compensation plans. You can have big money up front, big money at the back end, or moderate money throughout your career—but you can have only one.

So when you start thinking about compensation plans, ask yourself this question first: How would you as a distributor want the company to pay you? Big payout to those who are just beginning, big payout to those who have spent years building successful businesses, or a balanced amount for all involved?

Before you choose, know that there are good arguments for all three. When companies provide strong financial incentive in the beginning, a lot of people will join the organization; the down side of this is that these distributors might not have strong financial incentive to build large organizations or stay around for the long haul. The carrots won't grow large or sweet enough. When there's a strong financial incentive at the back end (for those higher in the organization), strong leaders will race to join. Trouble is, they may struggle to get less ambitious distributors to join.

And finally, although a balanced plan might sound best, it also might not be strong enough to attract those from either end.

Generally speaking, if you want money right from the start, your best bet is to choose a more traditional direct-sales company. A direct sales company will pay you commissions primarily for the sales you make and not so much for the sales made by those you bring into the business.

If you want unlimited opportunity and don't mind waiting for the payout, consider a stair step/breakaway program.

It offers you the chance to build both wide and deep (that is, have many people directly under you, each of which may have several layers under them as well). The downside of this structure is that you'll have a large organization to manage.

As you start to consider companies based on their compensation plan, look for a distributor who understands the plan. Ask them to explain it to you. You can get the name of a distributor by reading the company magazines or the industry magazines. Often e-mail addresses for specific distributors are listed.

Also, if money isn't your primary concern, you may want to simply trust the company's plan and focus on other factors in making your decision.

FIND A GREAT SPONSOR

Many distributors have succeeded without a strong sponsor. Even so, every successful distributor will tell you that this is one of the most important factors in their success. This one person, if she or he really understands the role, can help you learn the system faster, keep you motivated, smooth the rough spots, recognize your efforts, and more. Make no mistake: If you find a sponsor who's knowledgeable, supportive, dedicated, and a person of integrity, you will be well on your way to success.

This connection between distributor and sponsor is so important that you may choose to work with a company simply because you found an upline sponsor whose values and ambitions you shared. Margaret Tanaka, who now has a large Shaklee organization, says it never would have existed if it weren't for her sponsor, Barbara Lagoni. "Long before I had any confidence in myself, she was telling me that I was a born leader. Her belief in me and knowledge of this business were extremely powerful in the early years."

Your sponsor need not be someone who lives close by. Although this might initially seem important, it really matters more that the person can be a great resource. With the Internet and ever-lower long-distance telephone rates, you can connect with this person as often as necessary. In your search for a sponsor, place ability above proximity.

To find a great sponsor, start by reading the company's literature. Look for stories that resonate with you. Look for people with whom you think you have something in common. Make sure you find a person whose success is established. You can also call the company, speak to someone from sales, and ask for a referral. When you find someone who strikes you as having good sponsor potential, contact her or him through the company to see whether you have indeed found your match.

FIND A COMPANY THAT WILL SUPPORT YOU

A popular saying in network marketing is, *while you are in business for yourself, you are not in business by yourself.* Your parent company can offer immeasurable support. For a modest initial start-up fee (usually less than $500), you get access to the many things your business needs to grow: literature, forms, product samples, business aids, and more.

Another resource that a good company will offer you is a field development department. Here you'll get answers to many of the frequently asked questions, useful product information, and more.

Check to see whether the company's field support department has a toll-free number. Also try to place a call at different times to find out what the wait is likely to be.

The DSA's Web site will take you to many of their member companies' Web sites. This would be an excellent way to review and learn about many of the member companies in a relatively short time.

Remember, though, that although there are many, many long-standing corporate successes in network marketing (for example, Watkins, Avon, Mary Kay, and Shaklee), there are many others who have not or will not withstand the test of time. If the company you choose doesn't survive, you won't either. Neither you nor anyone else can look into the crystal ball to find out who will and who won't succeed. Nevertheless, the odds will always favor the well informed.

One of the first things you'll be exposed to is the company sales literature. As a distributor you'll need brochures, catalogs, order forms, and more to help you promote your business. Most often these items are sold to the distributors at a nominal cost. The design, writing, printing, scheduling—and most of all, the costs—are typically handled by the parent company. (If you've ever experienced the cost and stress of having something printed, you'll know that this alone is a wonderful benefit!) Even as a small business, you would have access to big business advantages—in this case, abundant and affordable high-quality literature.

Another tool your company will offer is training. (You should note that the best source for training information is your upline sponsor. But if you had the misfortune of signing up before you read this chapter, the company will usually make every effort to fill in the training gaps that your sponsor can't fill.) Your starter kit is typically your first exposure to the company's training materials. This kit might include a video or audio tape, and a number of sections within a three-ring binder that will help you better understand the products and the opportunity.

Final note: Remember that in love and in business, what first catches your eye is not usually what sustains your interest. (There are, of course, exceptions—such as Sandy Christensen, who fell in love with the Warm Spirit catalog and still loves the products!) Look for a quality organization that nurtures its distributors with intelligent and caring customer service representatives, high-quality training programs, progressive technology tools, and meaningful incentive programs.

Find a Company That You Can Support

Find out what the media is saying about the companies that interest you. And pay attention to the company's years in business and recent growth pattern.

Another bit of useful homework is to check the financial position of the companies that you're considering. You'll need to do a lot of sleuthing if the company is privately held; but if it's public, you can simply call them up and ask for a copy of their annual report or check to see if they have it posted on their Web site.

Find a Selling Process That Will Work for You

Essentially, you'll need to choose between two ways to get the word out about network marketing products: what's called the "party plan" and the person-to-person method. As with compensation plans, one isn't necessarily better than the other—they're just different ways for getting the job done.

With the party plan you'll be presenting to a larger group rather than to individuals. Also, you'll probably have some kind of host program in place so that someone else will be responsible for inviting the actual participants to attend. This allows you to shift your focus to finding hosts for several customers, rather than finding the customers themselves.

The party plan concept has existed for many years, but it seems especially popular today. Tupperware was one of the first companies to capitalize on its benefits. Now, The Pampered Chef, Longaberger, Home Culinarian, and many others have built their business around this women-friendly system for introducing others to new products and services.

With one-on-one sales, you're in charge of both finding the potential customers and giving the presentations to them. One of the advantages is that you have total personal contact and can customize your presentation according to the specific participant's needs. You may find yourself more comfortable conversing one-on-one than presenting to a group. On the other hand, you might find it easier to make fewer contacts and let these people recruit most of the actual customers.

Section III: Knowing What to Look <u>Out</u> For

WHEN MARGARET TANAKA started building her business, she heard a lot of horror stories—about people who had lost their farm trying to build a network marketing business, people with garages full of products they couldn't sell, people who became known as "the neighborhood pest" because of overzealous recruitment. Margaret realized that before she could build a business she needed to understand the industry better—its history, its mistakes, and its reinvention.

"John Kalench's *Being the Best You Can Be in Multilevel Marketing* was enormously helpful," Margaret says. "*Upline* magazine was also a good resource. And "The Woman's Tapes"—ordered through *Upline*—featured six female distributors who made it abundantly clear what the best of this industry is all about. Incredibly, the minute I understood our industry's shadowed past and felt comfortable talking about it, no one ever again asked me about it."

Although this chapter cannot replace the value of doing your own research, we can highlight some pitfalls you need to be aware of as you begin your search. Not all network marketing companies, and not all network marketers, build ethical businesses. The good news is that bright red flags fly over the unethical ones. With just the tiniest bit of homework, you can see 'em a mile away.

BRIGHT RED FLAG NUMBER 1: HOLLOW PRODUCTS

Products are the heart and soul of this business. Make no mistake about this: Without quality products and reasonable, competitive prices, you have nothing. When the product is both poor quality and expensive, you are looking at a business that's not likely to succeed. Ask yourself if you would still buy the product even if no opportunity was attached to it. If you wouldn't, then it's likely that your customers won't either. Find a company that offers real products at reasonable prices. This is what you can sell. This is what others will buy. And this is what builds your business.

Bright Red Flag Number 2: Skewed Compensation Plan

Look at the compensation plan. Are distributors compensated primarily for the sale of products or are they paid primarily for "bringing others in to the business?" Keep in mind that in all network marketing companies, recruiting others plays a large part in your success, but that doesn't mean it should be the primary source of funding for the company. If it is, you need to learn a little about the phrase "pyramid scheme." (See chapter 3 for a more detailed explanation.)

An excellent resource that can provide understanding of what is and is not pyramid is an audiotape series called "What to Look for and What to Look Out for in Multilevel Marketing," put together by Kevin Grimes, a partner in the law firm of Grimes & Reese, a company that provides legal services for many of the largest network marketing corporations. This three-tape program tells you the honest truth about pyramid schemes. Whether you're new, experienced, or training your recruits, you'll find this an invaluable source of a clear and legal definition of a pyramid. (See appendix 2 for ordering information.)

Bright Red Flag Number 3: Outlandish Claims

You know this old saying: "If it sounds too good to be true, it probably is." Should a recruiter ever tell you something that sounds wonderful but unbelievable, tell him your children are calling, tell him that you have a call waiting, tell him you simply aren't interested—or whatever you need to do to politely excuse yourself.

Here's a small sampling of some unreliable claims:

- "With Company X you will get rich quick."
- "You can quit your day job today."
- "This is a business that runs itself."
- "I'll build a downline for you."
- "All you have to do is give me names."
- "You won't have to sell a thing."

Network marketing is a sales business. The foundation for every single company in this industry is its products, and selling these products for profit takes a lot of hard work. No matter what they say, no one can build a business for you. Success does not happen overnight; it takes time and effort. If anyone tells you this, proceed with caution.

Susan Waitley can testify to the work *and rewards* involved in network marketing. "Though I've made a *very* full-time commitment to this business, in five years' time I've managed to make more than $1,000,000 and qualify for USANA's Million Dollar Club."

Word of Caution: Although you may be tempted to immediately jump ship and work your new network marketing business full time, don't do it. Hang on to your day job during your early months and give yourself time to build your organization on a part-time basis. Consider quitting your day job only when your network marketing income equals or surpasses your current income. As we've said before, network marketing business takes time to build.

Bright Red Flag Number 4: Voodoo Economics

There are three figures that you should key on immediately in your search for a quality network marketing company:

Product price
Cost of starter kit
Recommended upfront investment

If the product's retail price is too high, your business can never be centered on products because customers won't buy them. You may be able to sell them to those who are interested in the opportunity, but real customers simply won't buy them.

The cost of the basic starter kit materials should be less than $100. Business builder kits that include sample products or personal training may be more, but $100 should be the maximum for the literature and training materials you need to start your business.

Huge upfront investments may signal a pyramid. All companies want their distributors to use and understand the goods they're selling, which makes some initial investment necessary. Investment beyond this—what's necessary to learn about the products—may signal trouble.

Section IV: The 25 Most Important Questions to Ask Your Finalist Companies

At the beginning of this chapter we talked about making our best choices when we listen to our hearts, minds, and souls. Use the following 25 questions to help you acquire a more emotional feel for the company. The answers are meant only to give you *pieces* of the puzzle. There are other—perhaps even more important—questions to ask. For example, when you talk to the company representatives, read their literature, visit their Web site, how do you feel? Are you making a connection? Are you sensing quality, sincerity, and integrity? Are you feeling that this is a place where you'll find what you're looking for?

One of the best tools you have for selecting a company is your female intuition. This "inner vibe" will steer you toward the good and on into the great. Talk to it. Listen to it.

Products

1. What's the nature of the company's products? Consumables? Unique? High quality? Innovative? Marketable? Well priced? Competitive with retail brands? Used and needed by everyone?
2. What are the company's three best-selling products?
3. What's the average customer order size?
4. What's the company's product guarantee? What's the return policy?

Company

5. Who's running the company? What kind of person is she or he?
6. Is there a strong management team in place? (Research bios on Web sites or in company magazines or brochures.)
7. How long has the company been in business? What are its annual sales? What's the company's recent growth pattern?

8. Are their products sold internationally? If yes, where? If not, does the company have plans for international expansion?

9. Is the company a member of the Direct Selling Association?

Technology Issues

10. What's the company's Web site like? Does it provide customers with lots of great product and company information? Does it give you a feeling of depth and significance?

11. Can customers order products online? Can new recruits enroll online? Can customers ask online product questions? And how quickly will they deliver products to the customers?

Operational Issues

12. What are the hours of operation for the field development representative service department?

13. How are products delivered to customers?

14. Are shipping charges flat fees or are they based on location?

15. Where are its distribution centers? (A nearby distribution center may lower shipping costs and speed delivery times.)

Enrollment

16. What does it cost to sign up? What's included in the starter kit?

17. Is a new distributor required to purchase an unnecessary amount of the product?

Customer Base

18. How many distributors does it have?
19. Does the company have an average earnings chart for its distributor base? How many of them are earning monthly bonus checks?
20. Is there a program in place to encourage repeat business?

Distributor Programs and Incentives

21. Where have their last three conventions been held? What does it cost to attend a convention? Can you earn your way to the convention?
22. What about recognition programs? Incentive programs? Distributor training programs?

Compensation Plan

23. What's the commission on retail sales?
24. What kind of work effort is necessary to earn $500?
25. Where's the money? At the front? In the back? Or balanced throughout?

Let your heart, brain, and soul guide you through this journey. When they all align, you'll know your path to success awaits you. The choice is yours, so enjoy the process.

CHAPTER SIX

The Inside Scoop

Connecting with a Female-Friendly Company

S O MANY COMPANIES are missing the boat when it comes to marketing to women. Many think they are, when in fact they merely have "women's initiatives" rather than true female souls or cultures. Marketing to women is doubly important for direct selling and network marketing companies because they need to both offer products or services that women can be passionate about, and they must offer a business opportunity that both appeals to and supports women. Because every female soul is slightly different, and each individual has slightly different reasons why she wants to become part of a network marketing company, we will explore next how you can tell whether a company appeals to your female soul.

Because you are going to invest a lot of time building a business and relationships within that business, you want to find a company that appeals to you personally and about which you can be passionate. It may be the way a caring company is run, the charitable causes it supports, or the special events and touches they offer in recognition or travel-incentive programs. It may be something else, large or small, that fulfills your need. The companies we describe below recognize and seek to be soul mates to and welcoming harbors for women in search of a business opportunity.

Women in Company Management

BECAUSE WOMEN make up 73 percent of the field sales force, this gender bias should be reflected in internal management of direct selling or network marketing companies that sell women's products. In companies that sell mass appeal products and services (such as telecommunications or nutritional supplements), a management team more evenly balanced between men and women is appropriate. Check to see what roles and responsibilities women play in these organizations. In particular, women should work in the areas where the company develops its values and culture.

> WOMEN buy or influence the purchase of 80 percent of all consumer goods. Marketing to women is a big and echoing void.
>
> —Faith Popcorn,
> author of *EVEolution*

Because women make up such a high percentage of potential buyers and distributors, companies cannot afford to slight this group. Rather, they must learn to target and cater to them. The products, the opportunity, the marketing plan, and the process *must* appeal to women and meet their needs. To do this, a company needs a significant number of women in meaningful positions (on the "inside") who understand how a woman feels, how she thinks, and what is important to her.

Tom Peters, a very powerful and insightful "management guru" who understands excellence and the marketing process, says this: "Any [women's] strategy must include both sides of the coin: (1) the market opportunity and (2) the organizational capability associated with serving it imaginatively (e.g., percentage of women in senior positions)." In other words, the leadership and management of network marketing companies, and industry policymakers must mirror the high percentage of women distributors and consultants, or it will just be a woman's initiative, not a strategy that is capitalized upon. Without appropriate representation, women will not "own" the industry, but will merely "rent" it, and it will not be all that it could be.

> IT'S a woman's world. Women purchase/are purchasing agents for well over half the U.S. GDP (commercial & consumer goods). Almost no Big Co. "gets it". . . . It takes total transformation—not a "woman's initiative" to take advantage of this bizarrely neglected commercial opportunity.
>
> —Tom Peters, author of *The Circle of Innovation,* 1999

The good news is that some direct selling/network marketing corporations have made huge strides in recent years. In addition, many of the companies founded and still led by women have enjoyed enormous growth, so that female executive representation based on the size of a company, and the sales volume is improving.

Helping to sway the balance of representation were two major appointments in billion-dollar public companies that encompass a large number of distributors. In 1999, Andrea Jung was named the first female CEO of Avon Products,

Inc., and Christina Gold (formerly of Avon) was named vice chairman and CEO of Excel Communications. Avon does annual worldwide sales of $5.2 billion, and has over 3 million representatives worldwide, most of whom are women. Excel is a $1.23 billion business.

Mary Kay Inc., which has 600,000 consultants and does $2 billion sales worldwide, is still run on the principles and values of its founder and current chairman emeritus, Mary Kay Ash.

Growing companies founded and led by women include these:

The Pampered Chef, led by Doris Christopher (60,000 sales consultants; $600 million)

Creative Memories, led by Cheryl Lightle (49,000 consultants; $150 million-plus)

Weekenders, U.S.A., led by Rosemary Redmond (12,000 consultants; $100 million-plus)

The Longaberger Company, led by Tami Longaberger (60,000 salespeople; $850 million-plus)

Some other companies that have top female executives include:

TARRAH Cosmetics, led by Leslie Campbell as president and CEO

Stampin' Up, with Shelli Gardner as CEO

The Homemaker's Idea, with Madolyn J. Johnson as CEO

Country Peddlers, with Lisa J. Brandau as president and CEO

Nu Skin, U.S. recently installed Char Knox (who

worked formerly at Avon, Melaleuca, and Free-life), as their vice president of sales (she started as the general manager).

House of Lloyd hired Betty Palm (formerly president of Tupperware, U.S.) to be its president.

Shaklee has continued to recognize the contributions of the very capable Carol Hukari by extending her role and responsibilities.

USANA Health Sciences has promoted Peggie Pelosi (a former Nu Skin Blue Diamond) to vice president of network development, the person who has the most and most frequent contact with field distributors.

Other familiar companies with women presidents are Arbonne International (Rita Davenport), Longevity Network (Adi Song), and Cell Tech (Marta Kollman). Even *Upline* magazine has become friendlier toward women with the advent of Uma Outka as its editor-in-chief.

FEMALE-FRIENDLY COMPANY CULTURE

As a newcomer, you may not be able to easily see what network-marketing companies are doing that appeals to women. As we explore this aspect of the business, you'll learn to look for these various aspects as well as signs that the company is female-friendly. In this section, you'll discover:

- How to tell if a company has a "female soul" or is women-friendly
- What a company's mission statement says about it

- What founders' stories and company histories reveal
- Which women's programs and charitable causes various companies sponsor
- What kind of women-friendly recognition and award trips are offered
- What women executives have to say about the industry and its future
- Why new companies are choosing to enter the network-marketing channel

We'll start with several "company portraits" that illustrate what the company is about. Then you'll be provided a checklist that you can use to gauge how women-friendly a company truly is from the inside-out. The intent, mind you, is not to single out any companies as good or bad, or to look for "feminist-oriented" companies. Rather, we want you to learn by example how to recognize factors that indicate that a company is friendly toward women. You can then do your own research, determine which company resonates with you, and choose one that fits your path and direction.

Companies with a Female Soul

SOME COMPANIES ARE obviously about women, and others may not be as easily recognized as female-friendly. If a company sells mostly products for women (such as cosmetics, women's clothes, or women's skin-care products), you will probably perceive a feminine aura. Avon and Mary Kay Inc., products sold primarily to women, come to mind. Companies selling products that appeal to both genders (such as long-distance or Internet services and nutritional products) may not be obviously oriented toward either men or women. If you are passionate about one of these more generic products or services, you will need to dig a little deeper to uncover the existence of female-friendly ways. Also, if one of your "whys" for wanting to join a network marketing company is to meet other couples or single men, an all-female company won't fit your needs.

You can also find clues to help you determine whether a company is geared toward women by reading the mission statement and history. If a company was founded by a woman, it is quite likely designed to appeal to females. By looking at some of the stories of female founders, you will understand the rationale for this generalization. Let's start our review by looking at some sample companies and noting the evidence that they are female-friendly.

> AMERICAN women, by themselves, are in effect the largest 'national' economy on earth . . . larger than the entire (!) Japanese economy. . . . this 'Women's Thing' is . . . unmistakably in my opinion . . . economic Opportunity Number one for the foreseeable future.
>
> —Tom Peters, author of *The Circle of Innovation*, 1999

MARY KAY INC.

Mission Statement
"To Enrich Women's Lives"

The Founder's Story
(Derived from the biography in the company Web site)

In mid-1963, after a lengthy and successful career in direct sales (with another company), Mary Kay Ash retired—for a month. During that month, she decided to write a book to help women survive in the male-dominated business world. Sitting at her kitchen table, she made two lists; one contained the good things she had seen in companies for which she had worked and the other featured the things she thought could be improved. When she reviewed the lists, she realized that she had inadvertently created a marketing plan for a successful "dream company." With her life savings of $5,000, and the help of her son, she launched Mary Kay Cosmetics in September of 1963 in a 500-square-foot storefront with nine Independent Beauty Consultants. Mary Kay Ash's goal then, which still remains the same today, is "to provide women with an unlimited opportunity for personal and financial success."

> WE all have the same values and goals that Mary Kay passes on to us; which are: God first, family second, and career third.
>
> —Carolyn A. Ward, independent national sales director for Mary Kay Inc.

Female-Friendly Factors

Mary Kay Inc. uses the Golden Rule as the guiding philosophy and encourages employees and members of the independent sales force to arrange their lives so that God is their first priority, family second, and career third. While doing some consulting for the company, Angela attended several leadership seminars for independent field leaders from Mary Kay Inc. At each seminar, every attendee was given two elegant booklets, one entitled *Living the Golden Rule*, and the other, *Traditions*. The Golden Rule is very self-explanatory; *Traditions* included such topics as the Mary Kay Philosophy, The Go-Give Spirit, The Adoptee Program, and many others taught from a female heart.

Part of the tradition and long-standing popularity of the Mary Kay organization is its ability to make people feel special through recognition. Just find someone who has attended Mary Kay Inc.'s annual "Seminar" (usually between forty and fifty thousand consultants attend each year, so that shouldn't be too hard!), and they can fill you in.

> I N response to the question Who inspires you?:
> *Mary Kay and women who have strong beliefs and values.*
>
> —Kerry Lynn Buskirk, independent national sales director for Mary Kay, Inc.

In the book, *Mary Kay on People Management*, Mary Kay says whenever she meets someone, she tries to imagine them wearing an invisible sign that says: "Make Me Feel Important!" Responding to that sign has been her trademark in providing recognition that has helped to enhance the self-esteem of countless women.

In addition to these booklets, Mary Kay has published an autobiography that sold more than one million copies; *Mary Kay on People Management* was a best seller; and *You Can Have It All* achieved best-seller status within days of its publication. (The buying power of women strikes again!)

Some of the awards and honors given to Mary Kay include:

- One of "America's 25 Most Influential Women" (1985)
- Circle of Honor award (1989)
- Living Legend Award (1992)

- Election to Fortune Magazine's National Business Hall of Fame (1996)
- Lifetime Television's Most Outstanding Woman in Business in the 20th Century

Mary Kay Inc. was also featured in the first and second editions of the book, *The 100 Best Companies to Work for in America*, and in *Fortune Magazine's* 1998 listing of "The 100 Best Companies to Work for in America."

In 1996, after more than twenty years of fundraising in support of cancer research, the Mary Kay Ash Charitable Foundation was established. It serves as a nonprofit public foundation to fund research on cancer that affects women. To date, the Mary Kay Ash Charitable Foundation has awarded more than $2 million in grants to noted cancer researchers around the United States. These grants help advance diagnosis, prognosis, prevention, and treatment of all cancers that affect women.

The independent national sales directors, each of whom has earned between $1 million and $7 million in commissions during their careers with Mary Kay Inc., wanted to come up with the perfect gift for the Mary Kay Ash Charitable Foundation in honor of Mary Kay Ash. They created a book entitled *Paychecks of the Heart*, which is a collection of stories, memories, and experiences that gave greater meaning to their careers, and according to them had "more lasting value and a richer investment than money could ever bring." Not only did they preserve the "most valuable intangibles associated" with their Mary Kay Inc. careers, but they also donated a portion of the proceeds from the sale of the book to the foundation to help "put wings on the dream for a cure" for breast cancer.

To sum up the company culture of Mary Kay Inc., let's listen to what Russell Mack, executive vice president of global communications and public affairs, had to say in response to the question: What does Mary Kay Inc. offer that is attractive to women?

> Mary Kay's mission is to enrich women's lives. We help and encourage women to build a successful business while living a balanced life with faith, family, and career in harmony—a philosophy that continues to thrive after 37 years. The Mary Kay career offers wonderful opportunities for self-confidence and personal growth. It's a caring, supportive atmosphere that is really special.
>
> Mary Kay Inc., truly believes in mentoring women to success. Our company motivates our independent sales force by providing the tools necessary to grow a successful business. Most importantly, recognizing individual and team accomplishments is the ultimate form of motivation. As our Company's founder, Mary Kay Ash, has said: "Let people know that you appreciate them and their performance, and they'll respond by doing even better. Applause and the recognition it represents are among the world's most powerful forces."

CREATIVE MEMORIES

Mission Statement

Creative Memories believes in and teaches the importance of Preserving the Past, Enriching the Present, and Inspiring Hope for the Future. We offer a successful company that provides joy, dignity, and pride for Creative Memories Consultants and staff members."

The Founder's Story

Cheryl Lightle connected her adventure with Rhonda Anderson's inspiration to found Creative Memories. Their destined meeting lets them entitle their story, "Two women with a single vision." Cheryl says, "Creative Memories began, as we say, with 'The Call.'" Here's her story:

> I had spent my entire life within fifteen miles of where I was born in Southeast Ohio. After eleven years at home with my children, I applied for a job at The Antioch Company, a publishing company in Yellow Springs. I obtained a job in accounts receivable, and, over the years, my role continually changed. Eventually, I worked for the president of the company.
>
> In 1986, I moved to St. Cloud, Minnesota, to oversee sales and marketing at Holes-Webway, a small photo-album manufacturer that Antioch had saved from bankruptcy.
>
> I stepped in that truck and made up my mind that the rest of my life would be an adventure.
>
> As the new kid in town, I spent many a subzero night bundled up in my apartment poring over customer letters from long-time Webway users who were having difficulty finding [our] product during the bankruptcy. I was trying to figure out why consumer loyalty was so high. I knew there was a market niche there somewhere.
>
> In January 1987, I was working after-hours when the night bell alerted me to an incoming call. Rhonda Anderson, a Montana homemaker and mother of four, had preserved her family memories in keepsake albums since she was fifteen. So when her sister called and asked her to give a presentation on making albums to a local "Mothers of

Preschoolers" class, she accepted . . . reluctantly. She thought that everyone kept albums the way she did and that the participants would not be interested.

After her presentation, she realized that her message had touched the crowd—she was surrounded by people who kept their photographs and memorabilia in shoeboxes. Several of the moms even asked her to conduct presentations for their families and friends. Rhonda sought the advice of a lawyer friend to determine whether what she was doing was legal. He encouraged her to call the Webway company and share her experiences.

Upon returning home from the lawyer, Rhonda found a postcard from Webway that she thought stated her favorite album had been discontinued. Not realizing it was after hours, she called the corporate office. Rhonda was bound and determined to let that phone ring because she needed that particular album.

After several rings, I picked up the phone and said, "Thank you for calling Webway. I'm sorry, but customer service is closed. Can I take a message?"

Rhonda then told me about her presentations and how she couldn't believe that people kept their precious photographs in shoeboxes. I was fascinated by the story, and we started making plans.

The rest, of course, is history. We were two women with a single vision . . . that one day everyone would preserve their memories in something other than shoeboxes.

Female-Friendly Factors

Some of the charities that Creative Memories supports are the American Cancer Society, the American Red Cross (specifically its Disaster Relief Fund), and Habitat for Humanity.

The Pampered Chef

Mission Statement

We are committed to providing opportunities for individuals to develop their God-given talents and skills to their fullest potential for the benefit of themselves, their families, our customers, and the company.

We are dedicated to enhancing the quality of family life by providing quality kitchen products, supported by service and information for our consultants and customers.

Vision

At The Pampered Chef, we have a vision that someday families all around the world will know the joy and rewards of gathering together in the tradition of family mealtimes. To help make this vision a reality, we specialize in high-quality tools that make cooking quick, easy and fun.

The Founder's Story

Doris Christopher tells The Pampered Chef story:

> In 1980, I founded The Pampered Chef in the basement of my suburban Chicago home. A stay-at-home mom with two young daughters, I was looking for a way to re-enter the workforce and contribute to the family's income, maintaining family as my number-one priority.
>
> The Pampered Chef began with one basic concept: to offer professional-quality kitchen equipment directly to consumers through in-home cooking demonstrations performed by a sales force of "Kitchen Consultants."
>
> Twenty years later, The Pampered Chef is a $600 million, privately owned company occupying more than

800,000 square feet of office, distribution, and warehouse space in the Chicago area. The company's 60,000-plus Kitchen Consultants offer a product line of 150 kitchen tools to home cooks in the United States, Canada, the United Kingdom, and Germany, while enjoying the same flexible business opportunity I did in 1980.

The commitment to fostering entrepreneurship in women across the country is a part of the fabric of The Pampered Chef. The company's independent contractors organize, develop, and maintain their businesses according to their personal needs. They determine their own hours, goals, and [desired] levels of success. For example, many consultants elect to work part-time in order to pay for extras such as a family vacation; whereas other consultants, whose earnings are a major source of income, dedicate full-time hours to their businesses.

Female-Friendly Factors

Company Founder and President Doris Christopher believes there is a place at the table for everyone—even those suffering from hardship or in crisis. In 1991, Christopher expanded The Pampered Chef's mission to millions of hungry Americans with the creation of the national "Round-Up from the Heart" campaign. This collective effort between The Pampered Chef's consultants, customers, corporate employees, and the America's Second Harvest Food Bank Network has raised more than $4 million in only nine years, "helping set a place at the table for everyone" by donating money to food banks. A similar annual campaign was launched to benefit the Canadian Association of Food Banks, raising more than $115,000 for hungry Canadians its first year, 1999.

The company's recent partnership with the American Cancer Society (ACS) is a national effort to "Help Whip

Cancer." Funds generated through the sale of a special pink kitchen tool and through fund-raiser kitchen shows held during the month of May benefit the ACS breast cancer early detection programs.

The Pampered Chef and Doris Christopher have been featured in *Today's Chicago Woman* magazine, "100 Women Making a Difference," 1996; *Executive Female*, "The Scoop on Five Hot Home-Based Sales Companies," 1996; and many other magazines. Recently, Doris Christopher published a book called *Come to the Table . . . A Celebration of Family Life.* It's a wonderful reflection of traditions, togetherness, and times shared to pass on values to loved ones who gather around a family table. Angela personally gave a copy to her mom for Mother's Day to thank her for all the family times of coming to the table.

> THE Pampered Chef is great at offering a yearly Professional Development reimbursement for attending outside workshops. This keeps fresh ideas coming into your business.
>
> —Donna McDonald, The Pampered Chef

AVON PRODUCTS, INC.

Mission Statement/Axiom

The Company for Women; Celebrating Women; A History of Partnership with Women.

The Story

A man, David Hall McConnell, who was selling books door to door, founded Avon. The story goes that in order to get into homes, he offered perfume samples to the women who answered the door. Over time, he realized that the perfume had more appeal than the books, so he decided to start a perfume company that he called California Perfume Company. Even though it was 1886, Mr. McConnell was wise enough to know to select a lady, Mrs. P. F. E. Albee, as the company's first representative to launch the direct sales perfume company (this was thirty-four years before women had the right to vote!). In 1928 the company name was changed to Avon, which he selected because of the beauty he observed while visiting Shakespeare's birthplace at Stratford-upon-Avon.

As early as the 1950s, the company was positioning the opportunity for women through its "Ding-Dong, Avon Calling" television commercials. The Avon Lady earned her place in history through continued advertising and sales. We used to say, Chevrolet, apple pie, and the Avon Lady were about as American as you can get. References to the Avon Lady have been heard on such popular TV shows as *Seinfeld*.

In the late 1970s and throughout the 1980s, the door-to-door territory-based business became more difficult as women joined the outside workforce and were no longer at home for the knock. During this time, Avon went through a shift in identity and made its business model more contemporary in a way that would find women in the workplace, thus getting away from its strictly door-to-door territory model. In the 1990s, it came into its own, or rather it got back to its roots, as simply "a company for women."

Now opportunities for the traditional Avon selling plan (commission) are offered alongside a modern leadership plan, which features both commission and overrides on group production. Avon today has evolved into a $5.2 billion company operating with more than three million representatives in countries all around the globe.

Female-Friendly Factors

As a women's company, Avon boldly states that it has a higher percentage of women in management positions (89 percent) than any other Fortune 500 company, that 47 percent of the company's officers are women, and that five women sit on the board of directors. Avon has been a sponsor for the 1996 Summer Olympic Games, and the exclusive presenting sponsor of The Olympic Woman Exhibition. The Avon Women's Running program is committed to introducing women worldwide to fitness through such grassroots events as 10K runs and 5K walks on its Global Women's Circuit. Avon celebrates women through its annual Avon Women of Enterprise Awards, which honors the nation's top women business owners for their entrepreneurial spirit and achievement. Each year an Avon representative is included among the honorees.

> WHEN I was a District Manager with Avon, they started their own network marketing program called "Leadership." I helped roll out the program in my district and believed in the concept from the start. When I saw that some leadership representatives were earning more than I was, I decided to quit management and go back to being a representative."
>
> —Miki Crowl, Avon Leadership sales representative

Vondell McKenzie, an Avon Leadership sales representative from California, was selected as one of Avon's Women of Enterprise in 2000. As Vondell headed into her retirement years, she was eager to find financial freedom and started an Avon business with her husband. They helped to pioneer and build Avon's Leadership program. Vondell is one of Avon's most successful Leadership sales reps, motivating and training other women to excel in sales. She manages a $5.5 million business.

Avon's Breast Cancer Crusade generates funds through the sales of special crusade fund-raising (pink ribbon) products, and through a series of fund-raising walks, known as Avon Breast Cancer 3-Days. In the October issue of *O, The Oprah Magazine,* an ad asked readers to "sign up for our crusade," which showed one of the pink-ribbon products. The ad indicated that the campaign has already raised more than $80 million. Avon received recognition as the best company for female executives in America from *Working Woman* magazine.

EXCEL COMMUNICATIONS, INC.

Founder's Thoughts

(Excel Founder Kenny Troutt's thoughts on a better way to connect.)

"Never underestimate the power of the individual. One person can touch thousands and make a profound difference."

Female-Friendly Factors

To many, Excel may appear to be predominately a long-distance communications company, but the women leaders at Excel consider it a communications company, and women "excel" in communication. The services they sell include long-distance service, pagers, wireless, and Internet services.

Because these are not "women's" products in the same way that cosmetics, for example, are, Excel does not stand out instantly as a women's company. A closer look, though, shows that the women of Excel feel strongly about this ever-evolving female-friendly atmosphere. As mentioned earlier, a woman, Christina Gold, is the CEO. Multiple top independent field leaders are women, and the women at Excel network very well with one another.

A recent Excelebration (the annual national convention) featured a workshop called "Excelling from a Female Perspective." At this workshop, Diane Chapman, senior director, and Carol Totten, executive senior director, gave dynamic presentations on what it was like to be female and work in the network-marketing industry and how they achieve balance in their lives. They shared how their spouses tried to talk them out of doing it, and how they persevered to reach their dreams. Carol Totten's husband was so concerned about "MLM" (multi-level marketing) that he feared he would lose his job.

Well, guess what? If you watch TV, you have probably seen the Excel commercial featuring Carol and her husband, who eventually did leave his job—not because he lost it, but because Carol's Excel income allowed him to do so, and now he is home with his family. According to Carol, "For fourteen years my children never saw their father because he was always at work. I retired him from corporate America over three years ago. Because of Excel, he's home 24/7."

Angela Moore gives her perspective of the seminar:

> I had the privilege of talking to the two audiences of about 900 people at these Female Perspective workshops. I wanted to share information about this book and collect input from

the attendees. It was one of the most powerful audiences to whom I've ever spoken. These women (and some "evolved men" who came to learn more about how to work with the women in their organization) sent such positive vibes to me and to each of the other speakers that the energy was incredible. No one was sitting with arms crossed, looking bored—they didn't want to miss a word! It just reinforced to me the power of women to connect with one another.

This type of seminar was very effective, and all the questionnaires I got back asked for more and longer seminars. It let the women know they were important to the company, and it recognized their special needs in the business. It was a pretty female-friendly statement.

Some awards given out at the Excelebration in honor of women and giving back to society include the Joyce Nichols Perseverance Award in honor of one of Excel's first female full-time corporate employees. It is given to the Excel independent rep whose "never quit" attitude has helped them to persevere. Another award, the Excellence in Service Award, recognizes the Excel Rep who, through community and volunteer work, has demonstrated compassion and selfless commitment to others.

Another not-so-obvious female-friendly gesture was the dedication of the July 2000 issue of the *Communicator* (the monthly publication for Excel distributors) to single parents. Kenny Troutt, who was raised by a single mom (Mama Nadine, as he calls her), began the issue with a dedication that included such statements as, "I have always reserved great respect and admiration for the women and men whose responsibility it is to raise their children alone." Page after page in the issue showcases single moms and how they were able to take advantage of this network marketing opportunity to better their lives and those of their children.

USANA HEALTH SCIENCES

USANA Health Sciences offers nutritional supplements and personal care products, so their primary image is one of healthy lifestyles for both men and women. Their field sales force is more a balance of couples, and female- or male-owned businesses. Statistics show that women are the great majority of decision-makers both about health care and the purchase of over-the-counter drugs. Thus it follows logically that women would be likely advocates for nutritional supplements and for learning about and promoting healthy lifestyles for themselves and their families. Because USANA's products have mass appeal, and the company places a strong emphasis on scientific research, it may not be readily apparent on their Web site what they offer for women. Here's a look behind the scenes to show you what they do to appeal to women.

Female-Friendly Factors

A few years ago, Angela was working with USANA in preparation for its annual convention. Much to my surprise, one of the agenda items was activities for children. In a definite "actions-speak-louder-than-words" move, USANA provided athletes, care givers, and volunteers for structured children's sessions so that parents who wanted to bring their children along could enroll their youngsters in these activities. It was such an amazing undertaking. I admired this bold step. It turned out to be a great time for all, and many people, including single moms who otherwise would have been unable to attend, came and adored this concept! This is one of the most female- and family-friendly examples I have encountered. Way to go, USANA!

USANA also engaged a woman, the noted researcher Faith Popcorn, to address its annual convention audience in 2000. I have also learned that a very big event held in conjunction with the annual convention is a major Women's Conference to support women's needs. At this session, field leaders share their stories and tips on how to support each other, and they teach women how to build their businesses. According to Brett Blake, vice president of marketing for USANA Health Sciences, "It is almost as well attended as the general sessions, and both women and men attend."

> WOMEN rule! Men and women . . . don't buy for the same reasons. He simply wants the transaction to take place. She's interested in creating a relationship!"
>
> —Faith Popcorn,
> author of *Clicking*

Each year at the convention, USANA sponsors a run-and-walk for charity. The cause varies each year, but it always supports a health-related issue.

At the 1999 convention, USANA's top Distributor, Collette Van Reusen, whose daughter Lexi died after battling cystic fibrosis, and who has personally given tens of thousands of dollars to CF research, led USANA's charity walk to raise more money for cystic fibrosis research.

USANA also supports women through its research in the area of wellness. The Wentz Wellness Center in Atlanta was founded by gynecologists to focus on women's health issues and has expanded to include other research on nutrition.

INSIGHTS ON MORE COMPANIES

Weekenders USA

Their slogan is "Clothes you love to live in." They indicate that Weekenders USA, Inc. is a company designed to make shopping for women affordable, practical, and fun right in the comfort of their own homes." Rosemary Redmond, the company's president, says, "As a women's clothing company, we believe very strongly in the power of women helping women." Weekenders uses its Wings of Hope Pin to raise money for Y-ME, a nonprofit organization based in Chicago that provides education, information, referral, support, and hope to breast cancer patients, their families, and their friends.

Shaklee Cares

Shaklee Cares has given over $600,000 in cash and products to individual families and communities affected by the unpredictable forces of nature. Charlie Orr, a past president, said, "Shaklee Cares wants to be here for the long haul to help restore community health and help people rebuild lives." Shaklee Cares focuses on providing assistance to members of the Shaklee "family" and their communities.

On her successful approach to recruiting women to Shaklee, Distributor Margaret Tanaka says, "Connecting, asking questions, hearing a need and then sharing from the heart what I'm doing and that it may be a match for them. I ask their permission to send them information to evaluate. I send them a tape I made that has eight moms on it sharing why they love their Shaklee businesses. My hope is that they will relate to one of these moms."

Nu Skin

Nu Skin shouts "women" on its homepage and American Web site, and in its beautiful new consumer catalogs. Nu Skin has evolved into a company that is balancing its product offerings along with its opportunity appeal. It has added a new dimension called The Fountain Club that supports its distributors and allows consumers to be more a part of their community.

Nu Skin Distributor Marguerite Sung says, "I have found that letting women try the products first is the best approach [to recruiting]."

The Nu Skin Force for Good Foundation* combines profits from the sale of its Epoch product line, distributor donations, and corporate contributions. It has partnered with Stanford University Medical School to help eradicate *Epidermolysis Bullosa* (a deadly skin disease that affects children) and provided money to The Hunger Project and others. According to company literature, The Force for Good Foundation seeks to "enhance harmony between earth and its inhabitants."

Discovery Toys

Because this company sells educational toys for children, one would expect the Web site to be all about children using its product—and most of it is. But you'll find some unexpected mom-friendly things, too, such as a section called "Parenting Tips."

House of Lloyd

"Not just Christmas around the world" is a motto at House of Lloyd, as is "Have business, will travel." Travel is one

---

* Nu Skin's Force for Good campaign provides millions of dollars to charities around the world that concentrate on curing and improving medical skin conditions.

thing that many network marketing and direct selling companies offer that women love. The chance to get away and be waited on for a change has quite an appeal. House of Lloyd has long been known as a company that offers wonderful trips to exotic locations. Destinations for the year 2001 include Paris and Dijon, France; Honolulu, Hawaii; Montreaux, Switzerland; Beijing, China; and a Mediterranean cruise that stops in Sicily, Tunisia, Malta, Italy, Monaco, France, Spain, Morocco, and Gibraltar. In past years, House of Lloyd has also sent distributors to Australia and New Zealand; to Africa, on safari; to Athens and the Greek Isles on a cruise; and on and on. The trips alone could make this company worth a look!

Executive "Insiders" on Network Marketing

EVEN IF YOU do a lot of research on a company and observe it as closely as you can, it is still helpful to listen to what women in leadership positions at direct selling/network marketing companies have to say. By reading their personally provided thoughts that follow, you'll get real inside information about why they feel network marketing is a good choice for women, what their companies offer to attract women, how they see the future of the industry evolving, and other areas they felt were significant enough to comment about.

CHARLENE KNOX, VICE PRESIDENT OF SALES, NU SKIN U.S.

Without question, flexibility is the number one reason that network marketing is a good choice for women. The many roles that women juggle demand that their schedules be easy to change at a moment's notice. Women typically do not find enough support in the traditional corporate setting to balance career and home life. Network marketing offers women the opportunity to make a contribution based on their own choices. They are in control of the amount of time and effort that they put into the business. In the past decade women have been starting businesses at twice the rate of men. There are now over nine million women-owned businesses in the U.S. This speaks to the fact that women want more control over their work lives and responsibilities.

Network marketing allows women to maintain complete control of their professional lives while offering them the opportunity to be involved in a community of distributors and customers. The socialization factor that Network Marketing offers is very appealing to women because most women are, by nature, social creatures. They are constantly looking for ways to reach out, especially to other women, in all settings: the grocery store, the gym, the playground, the water cooler, etc. The success that is gained in Network Marketing is usually found through other people. It warms the heart to achieve success through others and to help others succeed, both traits that are inherent in Network Marketing. Women also like "cause supported" campaigns that are offered in some Network Marketing companies. The Nu Skin Force for Good campaign allows women to involve themselves in a greater good or non-monetary cause that allows them to make a worldly difference. Women feel good about themselves when they are enhancing other people's lives whether it be introducing a friend to a new business opportunity, introducing a customer to a new product or fighting for a worthy cause.

Women will influence the development of new and existing Network Marketing companies. To find success, companies will undoubtedly have to pay attention to the needs of women, both as distributors and customers. Choice will be an important part of focusing on women. Companies must provide a choice of product as well as a choice of how to buy and sell the product. Some distributors and customers will be attracted by the high-tech opportunity of the Internet while others will want to maintain personalized one-on-one contact. The important thing is that a choice exists so that the most amount of women are exposed to the right information. By allowing women to maintain control of how they operate their businesses, Network Marketing companies will see an increase in loyalty from their women customers. After all, women distributors know best what their women customers want and expect, and usually have the power to influence the customer's buying decisions.

DORIS CHRISTOPHER, FOUNDER AND PRESIDENT, THE PAMPERED CHEF

Network marketing offers women a flexible earning opportunity, helping them to achieve a healthy work/life balance. It allows women the opportunity to start and grow a business of their own without heavy start-up costs. Network marketing presents an opportunity without boundaries; there is no glass ceiling to hinder a woman's full potential.

The Pampered Chef brings families together by offering kitchen tools that help women (and men) get in and out of the kitchen fast. Our tools, tips, and recipes help make meal preparation quick, easy, and fun, allowing families more time to spend together around the table.

As a recent past chairperson of the Direct Selling Association, the trade association for the nation's direct sellers, I feel that direct selling is the career choice of the future. In today's "high-tech" society, people long for the "high-touch" quality of network marketing, both as a business opportunity and as a mode of consumption.

CHERYL LIGHTLE, PRESIDENT, CREATIVE MEMORIES

At Creative Memories, we continually promote our career opportunity as a chance for women to make money doing what they love. Quite simply, we offer a rewarding career for those who embrace and want to share the Creative Memories Mission of "preserving the past, enriching the present, and inspiring hope for the future" through the creation of keepsake family albums.

What does "rewarding" mean to us? Several things, really. First, network marketing gives women the luxury of putting family first. Their established business hours can fit into their family schedule rather than vice versa. This equates to being able to stay home with children during their formative years, being able to be home if someone is sick, being able to volunteer at the school and events of their family, being home when the bus drops the kids off at the end of the day.

The rewards also manifest themselves in the meaningful work that our consultants do. We teach people the importance of preserving their special stories for themselves and for future generations. We offer the researched product and information that supports current standards in long-term photo storage. We provide step-by-step guidance and instruction for completing albums. And, we recognize and reward others for their accomplishments.

Our consultants have helped grieving customers through a loss. They have built a sense of community by volunteering services with local organizations to preserve heritage. They have helped people with mountains of scattered photographs compile a detailed history of their lives.

Among consultants, they challenge, support, and recognize each other as women, as mothers, as business owners, to be the very best that they can be without compromising their values and beliefs.

Within their families, our consultants are proud to be role models who are engaged in meaningful work and are bringing home income to support the family's dreams and lifestyle.

Financial rewards are determined by the consultants' goals. For some, Creative Memories and network marketing opportunities allow women to accomplish short-term objectives . . . to buy an outfit a month, to be able to be generous during the holidays, to take the family on a once-in-a-lifetime vacation, to be able to re-roof the house without taking out a loan or charging it. These are very real scenarios that can easily be accomplished without dramatically impacting the lifestyle choices they have made. For others, Creative Memories is an exceptionally lucrative business opportunity with limitless income and professional development potential. Doctors, lawyers, speech pathologists . . . successful business women who love meaningful careers but may get burnt out with the grueling schedules . . . choose Creative Memories and network marketing opportunities, so they can continue to earn the income equivalent to, or exceeding, what they made in their previous careers while still being able to put their family first.

This growing trend of people embracing network marketing opportunities will continue. I view this as society searching for the high-touch aspect of personal service in a world that has become increasingly technological. While medical advancements, Internet proliferation, and telecommunication developments change at lightning speed, people are searching for personal interaction, support, encouragement. Network marketing provides this.

While we may embrace online banking, grocery shopping, and other forms of e-commerce, we still want to know someone out there cares about who we are and what we do. So, as consumers, whether we are investing in keepsake albums, cosmetics, kitchen utensils, baskets, or telecommunications, we want our consultants to know we are more than just a business transaction. We want to trust their guidance, their recommendations, their belief in product and services. We want to know they care about our purchasing decisions. This will become increasingly important as technology continues to keep us from face-to-face contact.

ROSEMARY REDMOND, PRESIDENT, WEEKENDERS USA, INC.

Rosemary Redmond says the following when asked why she feels network marketing is a good choice for women.

Flexibility of time. Women can work around children and family schedules. (According to the U.S. Census Bureau, the majority of women in the workforce have children under the age of 18 who need their care.)

No glass ceiling for income and advancement. Every woman, regardless of her education, experience, socio-economic background, age—and just about anything else you want to put on that list—has an opportunity to create very high income for herself. According to government statistics, the average income of women working 35 hours a week or more is $480 a week. Weekenders, according to those statistics, offers full-time income for part-time work. In fact, because of the income potential, Weekenders attracts many full-time career women. We have teachers, nurses, engineers, administrators, and executives in our sales manager group. We even have a former chief financial officer of a company.

Personal growth opportunity. Because each person advances at her own pace, there is no pressure to perform; nor is there pressure to "produce or lose your job." However, there is opportunity and training to gain skills and experience. As a result of the non-threatening, totally supportive culture at our company, many women find themselves acquiring skills and achieving results of which they never thought themselves capable. The high self-esteem and pride that this generates is a joy to behold.

Role model for children and families. In addition to personal growth and financial success, these women are giving their children the best gift possible—the example of independence and self-actualization.

Contribution. Another great satisfaction that comes from building a business is the contribution you make to other peoples' lives through the product and the earning opportunity.

Rosemary feels that in the case of Weekenders, these are some of the things that are attractive to women.

Product. Our product is women's clothing. So, they have the benefit of a wonderful wardrobe at cost as well as the fun and glamour of being in the fashion business.

Luxury incentive gifts like fine jewelry and travel. These rewards are chosen as part of a program to help women raise their "deserve level," which, in turn, helps them increase their business success.

Rewarding and fulfilling relationships. When a woman comes into Weekenders, one of the first things she comments on is how loving, supportive, and encouraging the other women in the company are. (Because our product is women's clothes, all of our sales people are women.) Weekenders truly does offer the legacy of women helping women. They rejoice in each other's success and help each other achieve it.

Weekenders has partnered with the Y-Me Breast Cancer Organization and through the sale of Wings Of Hope Pins and other fund-raising activities, has contributed over $130,000 to their organization.

LESLIE CAMPBELL, PRESIDENT AND CEO, TARRAH COSMETICS, INC.

Women are unique in the role they play as the heart of society and of the home. With more and more women wanting to stay home and raise their families, home-based businesses provide an opportunity to achieve a combined goal of being home with their families and still being able to develop a financially rewarding career.

The excellent training, motivation, and skill development associated with network marketing companies also provides women with a supportive atmosphere to further develop natural abilities and skills which can increase their sense of self-worth.

In comparison with the traditional job market, network marketing companies provide opportunities for women to develop and flourish in a positive, growth-oriented work environment where women are encouraged and rewarded for their efforts, goals, and desires. Too often in the corporate world, women do not support and mentor each other, while doing so is the norm in direct selling. As a result, women not only grow personally, they develop life-long friendships that sustain them spiritually.

TARRAH Cosmetics, Inc. offers women an opportunity to choose a level of success they are comfortable with in a caring, nurturing environment. Our strong marketing plan encourages success—we know of no other marketing plan that compensates as highly for helping others achieve their goals and dreams, and we believe it is important to reward activity that encourages growth in an organization.

Typically, women find the range and quality of our products; the idea of being their own boss; working flexible hours; determining the amount of income they want to earn; the gifts, promotional programs, incentives, and supportive environment of TARRAH to be an attractive combination.

As downsizing and closures continue to affect the traditional job market, we believe more and more women will begin to seek entrepreneurial opportunities that offer security and growth potential. We will continue to develop programs and training that significantly increase the success of our consultants in both their personal and professional lives.

The past few years have seen party plan selling growing at a faster rate than other direct-selling methods. We believe that a large part of this stems from a need to feel connected to others and to be pampered. In the age of high-tech, women still want high touch and our business offers that alongside an earning opportunity.

By recognizing certain trends in our society and working to accommodate them, we are building a company of convenience for women. For example, with the recent trend toward smaller living quarters we recognize that space is a premium—carrying inventory doesn't make sense and getting orders out quickly with short delivery times allows an apartment dweller to still operate a successful business.

As an executive in our industry, I have served on several DSA and DSEF committees and am currently serving as chairman of the DSA Awards Committee. I believe it is critical that executives from all of our companies support the efforts of our industry organization—with our time, our talents, and our financial resources. Although we may all operate quite differently, the public perception paints us all with the same brush and we need to ensure that painting results in a pleasing picture. We can only do that through our involvement and commitment to the ethical growth of our channel.

As a "middle-aged" company (our company was founded in 1973), we have a unique mix of longevity (over half of our managers with fifteen years or more in the company) and newness. A change of ownership and change of name in the last four years gives us the best of both worlds—a time-tested product line that customers love and a strong ethical foundation coupled with a dynamic marketing plan and a feeling of excitement and new beginnings.

We have recently begun supporting "Dress for Success of Palm Beach County." This organization helps abused women prepare to return to the workplace with wardrobe and makeup assistance, among other things. So far, we have contributed product and cash.

Why New Companies Choose Network Marketing

ONE GOOD INDICATION of whether a channel is attractive and growing, or falling from favor, is the number of new companies. The party plan is the fastest growing segment within the direct selling channel, and numerous companies are jumping on the bandwagon each week.

This next section provides you with some direct feedback from the leadership of companies that are new on the scene, still small enough to be considered startups, or those planning to open in the near future. They explain why they have chosen network marketing, how they incorporated their understanding of women, what their mission is, and why they think their company will appeal to women. They also explain how they plan to carry the torch of having a passionate purpose, developing a unique concept, and contributing to the greater good as part of their legacy. In addition to these companies, many other familiar names, such as Southern Living and the Body Shop (in the UK and Australia) have also chosen this channel to grow their businesses.

Newer Company Profiles

YOUR GENTLE SPIRIT: MARIELENA CIROLIA, PRESIDENT

We sell essential oils, diffusers, true aromatherapy products, fragrant candles, herbal bath/body/facial products, wind chimes . . . everything to soothe YOUR gentle spirit! Our target customer is anyone who is STRESSED OUT!!!!

For approximately twenty years I have been using essential oils for myself and my daughter, Kristin, and believe in their therapeutic abilities. Whenever you go into a health store—something may smell good, but there usually is no one there who can explain what, say, peppermint oil, is good for. So the customer usually walks away purchasing nothing and definitely learning nothing. By Your Gentle Spirit selling directly thru home/office demonstrations, we are able to help educate our customers as to what our products do—what is NOT in our products—and they can continually come back to us for answers they may need. We are very concerned with customer service and pride ourselves on that.

We are passionate about helping women to achieve their dreams, to retain their power, and to realize that there *is* enough out there for everyone if we would just help one another. I was a single parent for many, many years. I know only too well how it feels to try to juggle a job and a child. My daughter was my first priority, but we had to eat, too! So how do you work days when she's three and four and still at home, yet be able to stay with her? The answer came for me with a part-time job during the day (very part-time), and then I was introduced to a direct sales company, which allowed me to work a couple of nights a week when she was asleep. What a great concept and what a great feeling to know I earned what I put into the business.

I knew from that point on that that was the way to go for most moms, and I vowed from that point on that if I ever was blessed with enough good fortune to start my own company, that I would always offer women the chance to not have to choose between family life and a career—but rather afford them the opportunity to obtain both while feeling good about themselves and the products they would sell.

Years after working with a direct sales company and doing very well, I had an opportunity to go into business with a friend. The business was successful, but as the years went on, I wasn't fulfilled. The business made money—more than enough—but that was it. Period. Bills were paid, vacations taken, "things" bought. But I was empty on the inside. That's when I began questioning what I wanted to do with my life and how I would feel "filled up." I felt filled up when I left a soup kitchen or the Ronald McDonald House or helped out a homeless man buy clothes—so what could I do on an every-day level to help others?

That's when it hit me—direct sales—offer the opportunity to as many women (or men) who wanted the opportunity and what would I sell? Essential oils—something I had been using for many, many years and something everyone who knew me kept asking about . . . "What's good for my headaches?" . . . "lavender oil," "What will ease my stomachaches?" . . . "peppermint oil." Why not help answer questions while importing high-quality products, and we'll throw in great fragrant candles and bath products and we'll help relax everyone! Now, a name. What will I call this company? Something of a tribute to my daughter, who helped me through the darkest days (within months of my divorce, my mom passed away suddenly) and who was and is my gift from God. I had always said she was such a "gentle spirit," and thus the company name was born . . . for we all have a gentle side . . . it would be for all women . . . for *your* gentle spirit!

JS HomeStyle: Jill Sands, Chairman of the Board and Design Visionary

JS HomeStyle's official launch was March 1, 2000. Prior to this launch we conducted a 12-month test program. JS HomeStyle markets and distributes high-quality, lifestyle products for the home. We are on-trend, but not trendy. We are leading-edge, but not edgy. Our products and designs will become tomorrow's classics.

Our target customer is a female consumer with an age range of 25 and higher. We have found the median age to be 35. Women today have the luxury of choice not afforded to women in any other period of history. They have the option of career, family, or both, and we target to all three. We target to the customer who is choosing to stay home, raise her own children, yet wants the freedoms that her own business allows and we target to the customer who wants a fast-track direct selling career.

Direct selling allows us access to a mass consumer base while being able to protect our brand and margins. Direct selling offers us the most defendable market position of any distribution channel we have found. It allows us to control our brand, our profitability, and our future.

Beyond that, direct selling is a way to make a difference in people's lives. It allows us to use our products to change people's lives and the world in which we live. It gives women, specifically, the simultaneous freedom to be in business for themselves and to be home for their children. They can reap the rewards while we assume the majority of the risks.

Our passionate purpose is "Helping women to be in business for themselves, but never by themselves." Our

Mission is to help our consultants achieve their highest goals. Therefore, with the utmost integrity, principles, and high ideals, we are challenged to provide an environment of success so that women can attain their personal excellence. We are dedicated to sharing our vision and passion for making a difference in people's lives. JS HomeStyle . . . a "You-nique" way of life.

JS HomeStyle empowers women to enhance their lifestyles. We offer an enterprising Design Consultant Program and Career Plan in partnership with a product line that helps women create a home environment that is both personal and "You-nique." We emphasize that decorating a home is a journey and not a destination. Your home should tell a story about you and your family. A story about where you are, where you have been, and where you are going; the journey of your family.

Design Shows (parties) are the ultimate venue for the female-specific talent of multi-functioning. Women can:

- Socialize

- Get out of the house

- Have fun

- Buy products in a relaxed atmosphere

- Learn to beautify their homes with confidence

- Achieve personal fulfillment

- Launch an enriching and rewarding career

- Help a friend achieve personal fulfillment

- Help a friend launch an enriching and rewarding career

And, addressing today's time constraints . . . this can all be accomplished in two hours or less.

JS HomeStyle has donated a home to Habitat for Humanity and we have simultaneously issued a challenge to our design consultants that we will physically and financially help build a Habitat home in each of the 50 states. We will be working with Habitat for Humanity nationwide and in all local communities.

Additionally, we are donating a portion of the proceeds of a specifically designed product collection to a charity that offers care to patients with female cancers. We have plans to create design collections and donate proceeds to charities that offer care to patients of male-specific cancers and children's cancers.

It (JS HomeStyle) started with an idea . . . a dream to share our strengths, successes of experience, passion, vision, and proven products with others. JS HomeStyle was created to offer incredible opportunities to women, touching every part of their lives and empowering them to offer these same opportunities to others. JS HomeStyle is building a "You-nique," innovative, and exclusive identity placing us on the leading edge of the direct sales industry.

On August 6, 2000, we became the first Party Plan company to offer its full product catalog online for sale direct to consumers while allowing our design consultants to earn a commission plus full bonus value and full points. We will continue to leverage the strength of our design consultant network with the Internet, making sure that the design consultants are always paid for orders over the Web.

We are also planning to offer design consultants personal Web pages and access to all their business information. We will build and manage each design consultant's database for them, while providing them the tools to better utilize that data.

This supports design consultants in the fulfillment of their dream of entrepreneurship. We want to make it easy, fun, educational, and financially rewarding. We want to maximize the design consultants' rewards while minimizing their risks.

Finding Female-Friendly Companies

BY NOW YOU'RE more familiar with what network marketing is all about, and why it can be the very best opportunity for women. It's time to take action by exploring some of the many opportunities out there to see which is best for you. You can find out about various companies in several ways:

- Go to the company's Web site (usually www.companyname.com).
- Look at the print resources and company literature.
- Talk with a current or former consultant.
- If the company is publicly held, look at its annual report, which lists the officers and directors (and usually has a photo of the group).
- Call the company and ask questions.

The following checklist contains some of the questions we suggest you research when choosing a network marketing company. You may first want to make up a list of what is important to you and compare it to areas listed here. Then you can modify the list to meet your needs.

CHECKLIST

How does the corporate executive staff mirror the makeup of the field sales force (percent women)? The percent will be lower if the product is sold to both men and women, or if the field sales force is mixed women, men, and couples.

Was the company founded by a woman?

What does the Web site "feel" like when you open it—is it warm and friendly and does it seem as if it would appeal to women?

How do the company literature and communications materials look and feel? Do they appeal to you, and do they show women in the photos? How many top distributors or consultants are women?

What is the recognition program, and is the award jewelry appealing to you? (If the company only offers cuff links, it's probably not female-friendly.)

What kind of travel program is offered? Do you go alone or can you take your spouse or a friend?

What speakers have been featured at recent annual conventions? (If it's all sports figures and ex-military, it's unlikely to appeal to very many women.)

What causes does the company support? Does it champion causes that you feel are worthy? Are women's causes or sponsorships part of the company's support efforts?

If it's a public company, check out the photo of the board members—are there any women members? What's the percentage?

Does the company offer any special women's programs—networking sessions, workshops, baby-sitting during meetings?

By following the approach suggested in this chapter and doing your homework, you can select a company that works to enhance your life.

CHAPTER SEVEN

Virtual Office

Using Technology to Stay Connected

Y OU KNOW, IF Lois Lane had mastered all the technology that Clark Kent had at his disposal, she would have been Superwoman. I guess during that era, it just wasn't polite for a lady to change clothes in a telephone booth! Since then, most women seem to be on a quest to become Superwoman, but we're learning we can't do everything on our own. Today we have the same access to technology as do our male counterparts, and in many cases, the way we use these innovations has far surpassed the techno-founders' wildest dreams.

Listen to what a modern day "Lois Lane," in the form of Stephanie Stortz, an Excel independent rep, has to say about technology. Picture her walking around her home office in her techno-gear—a headset, a two-line cordless phone with all the bells and whistles, a beeper attached to her belt, and her computer standing ready nearby. Stortz tells us:

> I believe the technology available today makes it easier for me to work smarter. . . . Our business is all about commu-

nication. I could not live without voicemail, especially distribution lists. E-mail also allows me to talk to lots of people with one message. All of the new Wave Three technologies allow me to work my business smarter. The goal of my network marketing business is to work as smart as I can—to maximize the hours I spend at the business.

I begin each day on voicemail. I can train and leave motivational messages and general announcements to hundreds of people with one message. But I can also leave individual messages (answering specific questions, providing specific encouragement, etc.) through voicemail. I reserve "live" conversations to those handful of reps who I am working hard with at that particular time. This allows me to again maximize my time.

Voicemail is also an important part of my recruiting new reps. As I reach out with many methods—ads, flyers, "bump-intos"—all responses are filtered through my voicemail. This allows me to "sort" through and return calls promptly. (Urgent calls send a page to my beeper and I can respond immediately).

The Internet is becoming more important, although I have not mastered it yet. Fax on demand is something we have used in the past, but auto-responders for e-mail are beginning to replace them.

The Impact of Technology on Network Marketing

TECHNOLOGY HAS transformed homes across America and in doing so, has fueled the tremendous growth of home-based businesses. As such, network marketing has been positively impacted as a result of this evolution.

Never has it been easier to start your own network marketing business. Technology empowers individuals to work in a sophisticated, connected environment, in the privacy of their own homes. In this virtual workplace, women entrepreneurs can literally start a global business entity, wired around the clock and around the world via their phone, fax, and computer.

Carol Totten of Excel, for example, observes: "I have been able to build a multimillion-dollar global business from my home while raising my girls and never missing any of their activities while they were growing up."

In the early days of network marketing, consultants and distributors were stuck with the labor-intensive task of developing their own newsletters, then sending them by what we now refer to as "snail mail." They had to take possession of inventory to divide among their downline (those working under them) and deliver products directly to their customers. They had to guess which distributors in their organization had placed orders, calculate by hand who had progressed to the next promotional level, and worst of all, they had to calculate by hand the commission and bonus checks due to members of their organization. Then they had to write and mail each check to the recipient. What a royal pain!

Thankfully, those days are behind us. The technology that now supports administrative functions frees distributors up to focus on their main responsibilities: Finding customers (or in the case of party plan, finding hosts who will find customers) for the products or services they offer; and recruiting, training, and motivating other distributors.

While technology for technology's sake is immaterial, it's what technology allows you to *do* that's important. Think about it . . . new tools allow you to:

- Extend your office hours to 24/7 and let your business work for you while you sleep (more on this later).
- Work when it's convenient for you, regardless of time of day or varying time zones.
- Reach a large number of people with a single effort.
- Live wherever you want, and still stay "connected" to your company and downline.
- Manage your organization and easily monitor its activities.
- Create a professional newsletter at your desk.
- Connect with people all over the world.
- Create a professional presence on the Internet.
- Help others in the recruiting and training processes.

Marianna Panetta, an Excel representative, says she puts technology to work for her by "using my computer to create flyers and invitations to get people to see the opportunity." There's no doubt that such advanced technology can be useful, but it's not a requirement for a successful network marketer. The truth of the matter is that you can start a network marketing business with just a phone and a heart filled with passion, plus the natural gift of gab that many women are born with. Still, we're lucky enough to live in a century when so many technology tools are available, so why not use them? You can multitask to the max if you choose to, thus making the decision to develop a part- or full-time network marketing business both wise and very doable. These tools allow you to use your time and talents more effectively than ever before. And when you consider that the government will help you pay to create or upgrade your home office with the equipment and tools you need to support your business (through tax deductions—yes, you can write off legitimate business expenses), what more could you ask for?

The Top Ten High-Tech Tools

THE TECHNOLOGY THAT supports network marketing home-based businesses is a combination of corporate offerings and tools that the business owner brings to the table. Generally, you, the independent distributor/consultant, buy the equipment (although some companies offer incentives to earn certain business tools like Excel's recent free PC promotion).The company then offers specific business applications. The top ten tools that most independent reps vote for are:

The phone

Voicemail

Three-way conference calling

Corporate-sponsored messages that arrive by way of voice messages, conference calls, audio or videotapes, or CD-ROM.

E-mail (individual and broadcast messaging)

Corporate Web sites with company information and description of available opportunities

Access to administrative support/downline information from corporate offices

Personal homepages/rep home sites supported by the company and hot-linked into the corporate Web site and technical capabilities

Online ordering and processing of new rep applications

Fax on demand

This list is a combination of equipment, hardware, services, features, and software that allows you to best manage your time and the information you access through the Internet.

To be most effective in your home office, you need a phone with voicemail and three-way calling features, a TV/VCR and audiotape player, a computer with Internet access service, e-mail, a CD-ROM drive, and an all-in-one combination fax, printer, and copy machine. Most homes already have phones, TVs and VCRs, an audiotape player (may be in the car), and a computer. But even if you don't have all of them, you can get started with what you already have, and later you can progress to more sophisticated tools as your business grows.

In the later sections, I will explain how each of these tools supports your business. But first, let's explore some history and the link between technological development and home-based businesses.

It's Not Just the Internet

WHEN WE MENTION technology today, the first thing that comes to most minds is the Internet. While the Internet is hyped as the solution to almost everything, and is touted as the wave of the future, you'll use much broader technology in creating a network marketing business. Did you know that in the early 1900s after Thomas Edison secured over 1,000 patents (think about that residual income!) that there was talk of closing down the patent office, because "there was nothing left to invent"? Fortunately, that wasn't the case. Many things conceived and invented both before and after Mr. Edison's work have contributed to our ability to create home-based businesses such as a network marketing enterprise.

In his book *Megatrends,* published in 1982, John Naisbitt introduced the concept of high tech/high touch. He wisely said, "Whenever new technology is introduced into society, there must be a counterbalancing human response—that is, high touch—or the technology is rejected." He further noted, "We must learn to balance the material wonders of technology with the spiritual demands of our human nature." John Hess, in an article in *GEO* magazine titled "Computer Madness" adds this: "The error lies in thinking that new tools are the solution. It could be a fatal error."

As women, we know intuitively that any technology is only as good as the connections we make as we use it. We know that our strength lies in our ability to offer the compensatory high touch needed for balance in a high-tech society. Further, network marketing allows women to work from home yet be connected both to other women and to a major organization/corporate office without being controlled by either.

Telecommuting has, for some time, been viewed as the wave of the future. That future has begun. Indeed, some workers are already telecommuting, at least part time, but they still have not achieved the freedom implied by the phrase "working from home." One factor that was overlooked is that telecommuters, although working offsite, are still working for corporations and subject to their hierarchies and politics. Additionally, some people who work at home become isolated and don't meet their need for that high-touch connection.

Network marketing overcomes both these issues. It is a partner with technology and thus allows millions of women to work from home; be captains of their own industry and still have the full support of a corporate office back-shop; and by offering local training sessions, demonstration parties, regional meetings, and national conventions, women can choose to make the in-person high-touch connection with other women a reality.

Working at Home

WHILE TECHNOLOGY OFFERS marvelous opportunities to women who want to work from home, there are some caveats to consider when you are thinking about using your home as your workplace. One is that if you don't take control, your business can soon take over your home and life. Because the office is so convenient, you may be tempted to fall into "being at work" all the time. After a while, this becomes both exhausting and counterproductive to your *major* goals—spending more time with your loved ones and tending to yourself.

For this reason, if you work at home, establish a specific workplace and work hours. Your hours can be as short or as long as you like, and you can choose to work as few or as many days as you want. The point is that you, your family, and your organization should know when you are working and when you are off. Technology can help you here, too, by expanding your reach. Voicemail, an answering machine, fax, and e-mail will continue to monitor your business while you are off. You won't literally work around the clock, but neither will you lose sales or business when you're not physically on duty.

Stephanie Stortz, an Excel representative, is pleased with her home workplace. "I am most grateful for the freedom my network marketing business has given me. I choose when to wake up, eat my meals, do my household chores, and when to work. And all of that fits together! A typical morning for me is to get up around 8:30 A.M. and spend the morning in my bathrobe at my desk with my kitty on my lap! I have the freedom to work all day and not at all another day. I feel so blessed for these choices!"

Stephanie, like many of us who work at home, is a woman who is glad videoconferencing never took off. Remember that hilarious commercial about the lady who was loving working at home in her bathrobe and curlers enjoying all the technology, only to freak out at the idea of a video-conference with corporate invading her privacy? (Videoconferencing is one of those technologies obviously developed by men who don't know we aren't always dressed for success in the traditional way at home!)

Women would likely agree with John Naisbitt, who said, "Teleconferencing [via video] is so rational, it will never succeed."

Diane Chapman, an Excel independent representative, told me how she avoids the pitfall of keeping her business from taking over her life. Beyond establishing business hours, she has an agreement with her son that she will not take or place business calls from the time she picks him up at school (around 3 P.M.) until after 5 P.M. This is his "exclusive time," and it is time that she holds very dear. During these two hours, she lets her voicemail, e-mail, and messaging box do her work for her. On the rare occasion she really can't avoid an important business call during her son's exclusive time, she simply asks for his permission to make the call. His reply is generally, "Okay, but make it short," which reveals how precious this time with his mom is to him, too!

Despite the potential pitfalls of working at home, you can enjoy the huge advantage of avoiding the time, money, and headaches of participating in the ever-growing, road-rage-inducing rush hour. This alone can significantly reduce stress and free up time for more fun activities in your life. You can also choose to work virtually anywhere, which means you can live wherever you want (although it's best to start your business in a place where you have lots of contacts). You could move to accommodate other family needs, such as a transferring spouse or an aging parent.

Single people have the advantage of being in business for themselves but not by themselves. As a single person, you can always host or attend local training and opportunity meetings, host a party or workshop, or engage in activities with others in your group. These things can be a social outlet as well as a meaningful business-building activity.

Another Caution About Technology

As NOTED EARLIER, technology itself is not the solution, but the appropriate application of it is. Said another way, technology serves us, not the other way around. (Or, as the saying goes, it's a good servant but a bad master.) The whole reason we want technology is to expand our communications reach, to save time, and to help us work when we find it convenient.

Now, let's turn to some ways that technology can support you in the startup and ongoing efforts to build your own network marketing organization.

THE BASICS

Before you recoil in horror thinking about the money you might spend on equipment and office supplies, remember this: Tax laws allow for capital expenditure deductions when purchased in conjunction with business needs. We like to think of it as "sale" merchandise, because we mentally consider the amount of taxes we would have paid had we not bought the equipment. With this mindset, we can't afford *not* to invest in our business. Also keep in mind, though, that you must use the equipment exclusively for a home-based business before the entire allowance is valid. If you have enough space to have a dedicated home office—again, used for nothing but business—you can deduct percentages of utilities and the like, too.

As for the equipment itself, opinions vary on whether you need the more advanced equipment on the market. Everyone agrees, however, that the most basic technology tool needed in a network marketing business is a telephone. The following comments from network marketers emphasize the importance of this basic piece of equipment:

> I mostly (Major! Major! At least 2 to 3 hours) use the phone, although for saving time, I appreciate all the other technology.
>
> —KERRY LYNN BUSKIRK, MARY KAY INC.

> The phone is my life blood.
>
> —GRACE DULANEY, BIG PLANET

> The telephone is my business. I don't live near any of my customers or business partners anymore (since I relocated to the West Coast). I am on the phone at least 5 hours a day during the 3 days a week I work. I spend most of that time in accountability meetings/strategizing sessions with

my downline. I also do quite a few three-way calls with them and potential business partners.

—MARGARET TANAKA, SHAKLEE CORPORATION

One could hardly call the telephone modern technology, dating as it does back to 1876 when Alexander Graham Bell first transmitted sound over a wire. Yet more and more sophisticated features are continually added, and women have certainly learned to utilize this now-complex technology to its fullest. I once heard a story of someone whose financial history necessitated using a pay phone down the street from her home to start her network marketing business. I don't recommend this, but I definitely recommend you have access to a phone at home!

One-on-one calling is often considered the next best thing to being there. Although you cannot use all your senses to watch and see the other party's body language, you can be a sensitive listener to voice tone. This type of extra-careful calling is a must when you're first introducing yourself to a lead or handling a sensitive situation. A telephone call is the easiest way to have a two-way dialogue, get issues cleared up, and to answer questions.

Carolyn Ward, independent national sales director for Mary Kay Inc., adds another reason the phone works so well: "Nothing takes the place of personal one-on-one. I use my phone for communication. I have to 'hear' between the lines. My secretary uses the computer for almost everything. I do not. I need to hear the tone of the voice. I am in the "people" business. I will not replace communication with a computer."

Marguerite Sung of Nu Skin is another admirer of the telephone. "I find the telephone to be the most important tool in my business. It allows me to keep in *personal* contact with my distributors worldwide. On average, I spend three hours on the phone a day."

Having a phone line with a couple of added features on it and a good base phone set allows you to tap into the benefits of several of the top ten technology tools. These include voicemail, corporate-sponsored voice messages, conference calls, and three-way calling. If you have a fax machine, you can even tap in to fax on demand, and later you will be equipped to add Internet access.

The Benefits of Using Phone Technology

Voicemail is a tool that can allow you to have a professional presence and take messages from callers when you are not available. That all-important returned call from a prospect or potential host is worth the cost of keeping this service. Since you will (or should) set up specific office hours, voicemail can also free you up from answering the phone when you are "out of the office." An answering machine can also catch calls in your absence, but misses calls if you are on the phone.

Carolyn A. Ward tells of another use of the telephone: "I use a phone voice messaging system to get messages out to large groups." If you are on a system that creates a link to those in your organization who are on voicemail, or even one that allows you to organize broadcast groups for others on the same system, you can send information or motivational messages to a large group all at once. If you encourage your group to check voicemail frequently, you can use it to remind everyone of an upcoming training meeting you are hosting. You only have to do a broadcast message once, and at a time that's convenient for you, yet your entire organization will receive it, and do so at a time convenient for each individual.

A great way to use your phone to stay motivated is to access messages from the corporate office. An example of someone who offered daily messages for the field is Dallin Larsen of USANA. In his role as vice president of sales, each day he would leave a motivational message that USANA distributors could listen to by phone. Anyone in the field sales organization could access (or even broadcast) these messages for a quick pick-me-up. This can make the difference between a bad and good day, and can even save a distributor who might otherwise be isolated because her sponsor may be in another city or just isn't meeting her needs.

Karen Lameberson of Excel leaves comments on Excel's Telworks message system for the field: "Telworks keeps my business connected and inspired," she says.

Services offered by other companies include recorded messages, weekly conference calls hosted by company management, or a company sponsor whom representatives and their prospects can contact. The topics range from opportunity overviews to skills training.

Taking part in a sponsored call is also valuable if you have a prospect you'd like to have learn more about your company, to enhance their understanding of its credibility and the culture, or when you don't feel you can adequately answer all their questions. You feel like the whole company is behind you. Often, top field leaders will be on these calls, and you can tap into their expertise to support your efforts, too. Three-way calling works well in these cases because you can both listen, even if you are not in the same place. Betty Miles of Excel is one network marketer who makes use of this handy telephone feature. "I do many conference calls and three-way calls for my reps," she tells us.

You can also use three-way calling to get introductions from others who may have a contact for you who you cannot meet in person. When recruiting a prospect by phone, you can ask your company sponsor to be on the call, too. Later, when you have developed an organization, you can support the people who work with you by offering to be the third party in their recruiting or training calls.

PHONE OPTIONS

You know that you need at least one phone line. Beyond this single line, however, is a host of additional options that may or may not help you get started. They are:

- One line, no voicemail, answering machine
- One line, answering machine, two rings
- One line, voicemail
- One line, voicemail that answers and records messages when line is busy
- Second line, various options as listed above

If you're just starting out and don't have much of a budget, keep it simple. You'll need a phone with voicemail or an answering machine. If you can afford the separate number with the different ring (on the same line), get it. Voicemail is really no different from an answering machine if you are out, but voicemail offers the added feature of recording messages when your line is busy.

The location of your contacts (circle of influence) and your budget will dictate the type of phone and the number of lines and features you need. If you can afford it, I recommend that you get a separate phone and voicemail system to use for your business. That way your business is set up in a professional manner with a message geared toward business callers. Also, it enables you to more easily separate your business from your home life, as well as clarify personal versus business expenses for tax purposes.

You also need to think about whether you want to use a landline (plain old telephone) or a cellular/mobile phone. Although landlines cost less up front, you can now get some of the new wireless services (including wireless Internet access) at attractive prices. Some of these plans include services and features, such as long-distance minutes and voicemail, in the bundled price. Generally, on landlines, each feature is an add-on cost per month, and long-distance calls are charged in addition to the local access. Depending on where your contacts are, how you plan to build your organization (locally or in a remote location), and whether or not you need Internet access via your home phone or on the road, you're likely to find one option more appealing than the other.

Of course, a phone alone will not build your business, but it can support your efforts when you bring the right information to the table. One of the most precious tools you have is your contact list. This can be your personal telephone directory, your "little black book." Any other organizational lists you have in your possession may be equally useful—the phone list of soccer moms, the little league moms, carpooling parents, your church directory, and any other listing of clubs or groups to which you belong. You've accumulated this major asset over your life, and now is the time to put it to work for you.

To Fax or Not to Fax

If you have a basic phone line, you can add a fax machine for a relatively low cost. If you already have a computer with a modem and Internet access, you can skip the fax; because by installing a software package (i.e. Winfax), you can get most of the features and information you get on the fax right through your computer. You can even get free service to receive faxes via e-mail with efax (www.efax.com) or other similar services. If you don't yet have a computer, but you want to send or get information on paper quickly to or from someone, the fax may be a good interim solution.

Various companies allow reps to fax in orders and send applications in by fax to speed up the process. Other companies offer to distribute important information to their reps via fax on demand. This is a process in which companies assign document numbers (often the directory can be accessed from your fax), which you can request be sent to you over the fax. These documents may describe local meeting information, product information, third-party documentation about the company or its product, or other important information.

Other Basic Support Tools

In addition to your phone and contact list, you also need a day planner or calendar as a basic business tool. This doesn't fit into a high-tech tool category (unless you choose a Palm Pilot or similar electronic planner, or use a software program). But, to keep track of all your appointments, meetings, and other scheduled events, a basic paper calendar/day planner is essential.

Beyond that, if you have your car equipped with a cassette tape player and own a TV/VCR player, you can use them to listen, show, and watch educational and motivational tapes that your company sends. Once you have started your organization, or if you have access to or can afford more, you are ready to put other electronic tools to work for you.

Computers and Home-Based Business

MUCH AS WOMEN cornered the market in the use of the telephone, we are apparently doing likewise on the Internet. The number of women who use the Internet has surpassed the number of men. According to a study by Media Metrix/Jupiter Communications reported in *USA Today* (August 21, 2000), women account for approximately 50.4 percent of Web users and men 49.6 percent.

Anya Sacharow, coauthor of the study, says, "Women and men use the Web differently. Women are really pressed for time. They're juggling many demands. . . . For them, the Internet is really a productivity tool." He is later quoted as saying that men tend to be more interested in "technology for technology's sake" and that they spend more time online "just playing around" (when do we have time to do that??). Left brain versus right brain strikes again, not to mention the revelation of the long-known fact that women are the master multitaskers. It's not that we are all ADD, but we are generally juggling so many balls that it's no wonder we welcome the Internet to help us accomplish our many priorities!

A MATCH MADE IN CYBERSPACE

An astute observation on how the Internet and network marketing are meant for each other was provided by Bill

Gates, founder of Microsoft Corporation, who said, "Smart companies will combine Internet service and personal contact in programs that give their customers the benefits of both kinds of interaction." One could say he was predicting the new business model for network marketing—and your future success in the industry.

How Internet Technology Supports Network Marketing

If you don't have a home computer, it should be the next tool to add. With a computer and Internet access, you open the door to your virtual office and can reach unlimited administrative and marketing support for your network marketing business. You can then use e-mail; have access to your company's Web site and rep support tools, online ordering and application processing; and perhaps even have your own Web page.

Betty Miles of Excel is among those who find their own Web page a helpful tool. She tells us, "I have a Web site, www.bettymiles.com, that I set up to help my downline as well as many others."

Now don't get intimidated if you haven't yet touched a computer. (I say "yet" because I'm sure you will soon!) Author Angela Moore notes: My own mother, who has crossed the beautiful age of eighty (Sorry, Mom, I know it's not polite to tell a lady's age, but I need to make a point here!), received an IBM ThinkPad laptop computer for Mother's Day from my techno-brother Mel. She now uses e-mail to stay in contact with her six kids; twenty-six grandkids; and, as they get older, her many great-grandchildren.

Mom's certainly not the only one who has overcome "computer illiteracy." Carol Totten, a former housewife who is now an Excel leader, says, "Being educated over 30 years ago, I am computer illiterate; but I still manage to e-mail (to) a distribution of over 1,000 reps every morning with a training newsletter."

E-Mail

Truly a top time-saver, e-mail is now a way of communicating that many of us cannot imagine doing without. This book would have taken at least six months longer to complete had we found it necessary to rely on traditional mail to contact women in the industry, then receive the information they shared with us. E-mail enables you to write a quick note when the mood strikes you, and send it to any number of people simultaneously—without having to search for addresses and stamps—and it allows recipients to read it almost immediately or at their convenience. Think of how much more productive you can be after you put the kids down at night, or before they get up, or even during a sleepless night when you can sit down at your computer and do some magic.

Excel Representative Nancy Harms prefers e-mail over the interruption of a telephone call. She states: "E-mail (the flow of knowledge and inspiration and energy) is a part of my daily business process. I love the aspect that, unlike a telephone call, e-mail communication is non-intrusive."

Angela Moore notes:

Electronic communication is also essential if you expand your business beyond your town. I didn't imagine that my consulting practice would become international; but when you service the network marketing industry, it just happens. Thanks to e-mail, I was able to communicate with

CEOs and perform assignments as far away as Slovenia and Croatia. I have received comments about my first book and inquiries for service from Iceland, India, Mexico, and many other places where people would not have tried to contact me in the absence of e-mail.

I was asked to teach a one-day class about network marketing at the University of California at Berkeley more than a year ago. The attendees were described to me as a group of international business people who were coming from Asia to the United States. Upon introductions at the class, to my delight, I learned it was a group of top distributors from Nu Skin, who came to learn about all aspects of how business is conducted in the United States. They were extremely astute business people, and the group included a number of wonderful women. Their Blue Diamond leader, Miss Helen, who was a great company sponsor, organized the trip. One of the attendees, Vivian Hall, still keeps us all connected because e-mail makes it so easy.

E-mail also makes it much easier and cheaper to reach a large number of people. Formerly, newsletters and other written communication had to be produced, printed, stamped, and mailed. Today, using e-mail, you can blast out hundreds and even thousands of these same communications pieces, without any incremental cost of money or time. Think of the power this puts at your fingertips.

When asked if she communicates often through e-mail, Grace Dulaney of Big Planet responded,

That would be an understatement! Fortunately two and a half years ago, as we launched, I began building a huge distribution list that now reaches just about every Big Planet representative, whether they are in my downline or not. It is a highly effective mode of communication because it leaves people with a written record. Some find it hard to express urgent emotion in an e-mail, but I think if you can hone your writing skills, it is highly effective. The ability for people to be able to pass your messages on to their groups is also helpful. Women can use their days to effectively prospect on the phone and off-hours to handle other elements of the business through e-mail.

CORPORATE SUPPORT

The Internet has also become a major source of corporate support for company reps. In an area of corporate Web sites entitled "For Reps Only" or "Distributor Support," many companies offer important updates and recaps of current marketing promotions. Further, many allow you to access your downline reports to see how members of your organization are doing. The more sophisticated sites even let you tune in to the national convention with only a slight delay in the broadcast. Some companies provide basic services at no cost to distributors, while others charge for more enhanced services. The minimal fee charged is peanuts compared to the time saved and value received in return.

With up-to-date information from the people in your organization, you can immediately see the status of your business, including the impact that various activities may have on your monthly commission and bonus checks. Crystal Wilkerson of Excel is among the many network marketers who find the Internet an invaluable tool. "I can make contacts with the reps a lot quicker, and stay abreast with all the (company) information a lot quicker also," she says.

Information on who has placed orders during a qualification period, who has been promoted to the next level, who is not performing or may be just missing a goal, and the like is generally available. From this information, you can take the appropriate action to keep your business in top running order. You basically have access to the monster back-shop computer used by your company to track the activities of your organization. This really puts you in control. As Susan Waitley of USANA says, "Our downline management program allows me to keep a finger on the pulse of my business in detail."

Most corporate Web sites also allow you to have access to a professional business opportunity presentation. When you are sponsoring people who are geographically distant from you, you can use this as a reference, or the individuals on each end of the phone can work through the presentation on their respective computers. Those with a laptop can take this tool along when visiting a prospect in person, and display the presentation. Michele Gent of Excel finds it useful when she can't get to customers quickly enough. She shares, "When I find it difficult to set immediate appointments, I refer people to the (corporate) Web site."

When you have completed the presentation and the prospect is ready to sign up, companies with online application processes allow the prospective rep to enroll by way of the Web site and get started right away. To facilitate this and similar transactions, Congress passed a bill in 2000 that makes electronic signatures valid. The bill, officially known as the Electronic Signatures in Global and National Commerce Act, gives electronic signatures and documents the same force in law as those done with ink on paper. Putting in your applications over the Web can also have side benefits, such as speeding up your ability to advance. Kathleen Rayhawk of Excel says that her "Web site for signing up reps helped me get what was necessary to go to Senior Rep." Others in the network marketing business echo her comments and note, too, that Web sites have greatly reduced their paperwork.

Using online ordering, new reps' own first orders can be entered on the spot, which concludes the sale without further ado. This is a real time-saver for both the rep and the prospect! "I now use the Internet to place orders to the company and to send messages to business associates," says Valeria J. Bagnol, national sales director for Mary Kay Inc.

Rep Homepages and E-Commerce

We are now in the age of global garage sales! Such sites as E-Bay and Yahoo Action are letting us take one of our oldest traditions right to the world. If you have collectibles or other useable items to sell, by using one of these public sites, you can offer them across the country to millions of potential buyers whom you could not reach in your neighborhood. These companies then take a percentage (commission or override) on each sale made on their site. I like to think of this as a reverse network marketing approach because the company gets a percentage of every sale rather than the individual getting a commission on her own sales and overrides on sales completed by their organization.

Imagine how you can put technology to work for you by having your own home page or Web site where your customers can place orders directly with the company, with the commission coming to you. In order to protect the company trademarks and image, good companies provide their reps with a template to help them create a professional Web site that has links or connects to the corporate site. This is the gateway to all the complex software and security programs necessary to process private information such as applications and credit card sales. Usually companies charge a monthly fee that covers the Web site. Once the site is up, reps have a global presence, and a "storefront" that is open all day, every day.

Grace Dulaney of Big Planet describes her dependence on the Internet:

> It is an integral part of my business as my Web site is not only one of our products, it also is a resource of training and meeting information for reps and product and business information for prospects. It gives me a tremendous ability to leverage my time!
>
> The Internet has given us the ability to network with the click of the mouse on a worldwide scale; it is causing business to grow more rapidly as communication is instantaneous. The role of the Internet will continue to grow as the Internet itself penetrates the mass market. Devices like our iPhone (an Internet appliance that connects people to the Internet and e-mail without a computer) will enable the mass market to not only benefit from the Internet as consumers but also jump into a twenty-first century business without the need for technical skills.

In addition to allowing reps and their customers to purchase products and services offered by the network marketing company itself, some companies have created strategic alliances with other vendors to expand the store offering. Vendors in an alliance can be as diverse as Amazon.com, Lands' End, or even J.C. Penney (Excel offers these along with 700 other vendors). With this option available, distributors can earn commission or bonus points on additional product or service orders placed by their customers to any affiliate vendor. If your customers live in different time zones or place orders throughout the night, you can literally sleep on the job and continue to earn income. What other jobs let you do this?

The Future

WHILE SOMEONE IN the patent office may be again toying with the idea that everything that could possibly be invented has been, we all know that there is more to come. With technology, there are always early adapters who want to be first to have all the latest toys, then the early trend followers get with the program, and finally the mass market adapts to the most appealing products. So although many of us are now catching on to basic technology, another group is working on cutting-edge technology that we will someday use.

Some of these current arrivals include electronic business cards, smaller Internet appliances, wireless Internet service, interconnecting Palm Pilots, private chat rooms hosted by companies or leaders, direct deposit of commission checks, and other enhancements.

No matter where you fall in the timeline of technology, remember that technology is designed to enhance your business, not to replace you and your personal contact. Be careful not to hide behind technology just because it seems easier to e-mail a prospect than to face rejection from a personal call, or to buy an e-mail list and "spam" a lot of unsuspecting people because you're afraid to approach those you know. In addition, be cautious not to misuse technology by bombarding a prospect or a representative you've sponsored; you must be courteous and respectful of their time.

To avoid misuse of e-mail, Nancy Harms of Excel offers this insight:

> I try to be respectful of those to whom I send e-mail by clearly identifying the topic in the subject line! In this way, the recipient can tell at a glance if I'm sharing a "Business Building Tip," "News You Can Use," or if I'm requesting assistance, a response, or participation. I also am careful to use the BCC (blind carbon copy) feature on all my e-mails. If someone has shared their e-dress with me, that doesn't mean they want me to share it with three or 3,000 others!

The number one competitive advantage of any network marketing company is its distributors. The personal connection that distributors have with their customers and contacts is the secret weapon that makes this relationship-based selling process work.

Never has there been a better time to start a home-based network marketing business. The technological advancements over the last ten years have enhanced the appeal of this business opportunity. You can be a part-time or full-time consultant/rep for the company of your choice, and know that working from home is just a virtual nanosecond from becoming a global enterprise!

Yes, Clark, Lois is well on her way to becoming Superwoman!

CHAPTER EIGHT

30 Days' Worth of Network Marketing Wisdom

a.k.a. Qualities for Success

S OMEWHERE ALONG THE WAY the word "ambition" got a bum rap. Say "ambition" and we think "blind ambition" and picture a corporate raider, a dishonest politician, a too-vain movie star. But ambition is really about something honorable and human—especially in network marketing. Ambition is the simple desire to improve one's life. It's ambition that moves a mother to look for a way to work from home so she can meet financial goals while giving her child the best of care. It's ambition that drives the weary corporate executive to find a way to bring balance into her life. It's ambition that stirs the stay-at-home mom to pay for this year's family vacation. And in network marketing, ambition is not only a good thing; it's where all success is born.

Success in network marketing is formed and shaped through life experiences that happen long before you sign a distributor application. "Initially it wasn't my skills or my talent that built my business," says Miki Crowl, "it was the desire to succeed. When I was just beginning, I put together a scrapbook—visual images of the things I wanted from life: My family going to Disney World, a van with leather seats, a condo on the ocean. On the days when the going got tough, those pictures got me going."

What network marketers like to say about success in the business is that it's simple but not easy. What's "simple" is the process: Telling people about the products you love and teaching others to do the same. What's "not easy" is mastering the skills and establishing the determination and belief in yourself that you'll need to do those simple things.

Like all great life journeys, the process of building a successful network marketing business is a journey of never-ending self-growth. Although your journey will last much longer than thirty days, we offer thirty principles for success in network marketing that you can absorb by focusing on one a day for your first thirty days. Read these time-tested nuggets of network marketing wisdom as you wish—all at once or one per day. And come back to them again and again. Your success will take time. It will ask you to be determined, to grow, and to be patient. And know that each and every day that you work your business, you will become more than you were the day before. More knowledgeable, more confident, more savvy, more aware, more interested in others, and more available to others—even more available to yourself.

Day One: Follow Your Heart

No question about it, network marketing requires a leap of faith. Not a financial one, but an emotional one. You'll have fears. You'll face rejection. Your mother will worry. Your father will frown. And your friends may think you're crazy. But you will have to know in your heart that this is a direction that can take you to where you want to be. Only those who listen to their inner heart will find the courage to make the leap.

So listen to your heart. Nourish it by reading lots of stories about those who have gone before you. Shield it from the nay-sayers. Feed it with images of where you want to go. As network marketers like to say . . . a year from now you'll feel one of two things: glad you made the leap or sorry you didn't make the leap.

Day Two: Learn the Art of Self-Doubt Management

WENDY WASSERSTEIN, the well-known playwright, used to wonder what her mother said to her son that she forgot to say to her daughter—because Wendy's brother was loaded with self-confidence whereas she never was. Whether self-doubt is a mostly female quality or not, it's important—especially if you want to build a network marketing business—to tame the hungry, ugly beast.

Self-doubt has a life of its own. It haunts the talented, the skilled, the beautiful—even the most perfect among us can be plagued with self-doubt. And therein lies its weakness. Self-doubt is something we create. We're not born doubting our abilities. It isn't rooted in reality. It's disruptive software we installed into our own personal computers. And there's software that will get rid of it, too. Learn and practice the art of affirmation. Create positive, descriptive statements about yourself. Look your fears in the face. Focus on your goals and let go of your fears. Reprogram your thinking so that the only hurdles you'll face in the business are the external ones. You can do it and once you have . . . Look out, Momma!

Day Three: Live with a Pencil

IF YOU DID A cost-benefit analysis on all of the tools that a network marketer uses (business cards, telephone, computer, brochures, tapes, videos, voicemail, fax on demand and more), you'd surely find out that nothing beats the tremendous value and tiny cost of a pencil.

Write down your goals. Make them specific, measurable, realistic, dated, positive, and action-oriented. Keep them front and center. Read them a lot. And chase after them like there's no tomorrow.

Also, build and write down a list of prospects. Think of all the people you know who might be interested in this business: friends; neighbors; people with whom you do business, work, go to church. Use this list to start your business and keep it active by asking for referrals and continually adding new names.

Write a personal mission statement, a vision statement. Make a list of affirmations. The point is, keep a pencil handy and use it often. It's one of the best tools you'll ever own.

Day Four: Use Your Eraser

ANOTHER REASON to love a pencil is that it comes with an eraser. As we've already said, the journey of network marketing involves growth and learning. Surely you will discover new things along the way. Be prepared to change your thinking—and to change your goals to match that thinking. Be open to these new ideas. Be flexible. No one has it completely right from the beginning. Don't let old thinking get in the way of new and improved thinking.

Day Five: Have Passion and Passionate Energy

IN NETWORK MARKETING, you'll need both passion and passionate energy. The passion part is easy because network marketing companies offer some of the world's best products—wonderful things that hardly anyone has ever heard of before: plant-based progesterones that support a woman's chemistry, cookware with a thermometer on the lid so you know that your food is cooking at the best possible temperature, a drink mix that helps support arthritic joints. The point is, you can find lots of great products if you look a bit. Find products that you love and the passion for sharing them will come naturally.

And once you have the passion, the passionate energy is easy, too. Telling others about products that you're passionate about is not only easy; it's fun. And people will love you for sharing them. Seize the power of your inner passion; it's an excellent antidote to fear.

Day Six: Feeling Nervous? Congratulations!

AS ANY NETWORK MARKETER will tell you, the difference between a racehorse and cow is nervousness. Nervousness is a good thing. Nervousness is a signal that you're performing at the outer limits of your ability rather than staying calmly within your comfort zone. It's a signal that you're growing, expanding your boundaries, and getting better. It's a signal that you're doing something that matters. Learn to feel good about being nervous, and to put some of that "nervous energy" to work!

Day Seven: Ready, Fire, Aim

THERE'S A TENDENCY among new network marketers to assume that with more training, more practice, more in-depth product knowledge, they'll be better prepared. Yes and no. Learning more about your business and your products is always a good thing. But there's also something hugely powerful about plain ol' rookie enthusiasm—coming from someone who just loves the products and speaks straight from the heart. A polished presentation may be what you want to give, but a passionate presentation is what your customers want to hear.

As a network marketer you'll find your success not inside a book, or in a special leadership seminar, but in experiencing and learning from that actual meeting or party or workshop with prospects and customers. Don't let your perceived need for ever-more training get in the way of building a successful business.

Day Eight: Prepare, Prepare, Prepare

IF THIS ADVICE seems to fly in the face of the advice just given, you're right—it does. The last item was written for those who can't seem to get enough training and this one is written for those of you who think you can wing it—you can't. Here is a bare minimum list of what you'll need before you go out to make a first presentation:

- *Product Knowledge.* You've used the products or service and you know a lot about what makes them special.

- *Upline Experience.* You've been to at least three upline presentations so you have a presentation clearly in your mind.
- *Dress Rehearsal.* You've made your own presentation to a friend or family member at least three times.

Day Nine: Expect to Stumble

THINK ABOUT the day a baby becomes a toddler and starts to walk. Those first wobbly steps make our hearts sing. "She's learning to walk," we shriek. And yet as adults we never allow ourselves such a learning curve. We seem to think we should know everything about everything. Is this realistic? Of course not! Cut yourself some slack and expect to stumble. When you do, rather than give up, get up and try again. You're guaranteed to become more adept with practice.

Day Ten: Embrace Failure

THE DIFFERENCE BETWEEN an average distributor and a great one lies largely in the way she feels about failure. The average distributor fears failure, avoids failure, and always feels completely responsible for the failure. For her, failure is an ending rather than just a bump in the road. The great distributor, on the other hand, *expects* failure, *learns* from failure, *finds the benefit* in her failure, and most of all, *becomes better* because of her failure. And in time she moves far beyond any failure she might have once experienced.

Marguerite Sung says she made 100 crummy presentations before she made her first really good one. But after each presentation she knew she was one less "goof" from where she wanted to be. Today, she has one of the largest network marketing organizations in the world.

Day Eleven: W.W.T.T. Is a Four-Letter Word

W.W.T.T. STANDS FOR What Will They Think? And in network marketing it's a four-letter word. By being preoccupied with what others might think, we stop progressing. The fear of "What will they think?" stops us from doing what will make us successful. And when we stop doing that, we lose out on the important experience and lessons that enable us to grow.

Margaret Tanaka had recently begun her Shaklee business, selling nutritional supplements when a woman in her prenatal class called out, "Does anybody know of a good prenatal supplement? The one I'm using stinks." What more perfect question could any distributor be asked? But Margaret was so terrified of what the woman might have thought about her that she opted to keep her mouth shut. "Sometimes," Margaret says, "we're too hung up on our insecurities to be able to help someone else."

Susan Waitley, on the other hand, had severe stomach problems. Sometimes the pain was so bad, she could barely make it to the doctor's office, and the visits she did make to her doctor were unproductive. She started using USANA supplements and began to notice improvements. "When traditional medicine has no solutions to offer, and you finally find something that works, you want to tell the world about it."

Day Twelve: Find a Partner, Coach, Mentor

PARTNERING IS A powerful concept. You'll get more done. You'll learn new tricks. You'll have more fun. You'll have someone to share your victories with, plus a shoulder to cry on. Find someone whose energy and goals are similar to your own. Be open to all possibilities—perhaps an upline manager, a leader in another organization, a new distributor who's as excited about the business as you are. The point is, find someone and realize her powers.

"I knew I needed a mentor, but I didn't have one in my upline organization," Karen Hagen of Watkins says. "Then I remembered a woman from the corporate world whose style and attitudes I admired. I simply modeled myself after her, and it worked. I followed her approach, even though we were in different fields, and my business was better for it."

Day Thirteen: Lips Are Good; Ears Are Better

BEING ABLE TO TELL a sincere and engaging story about what brought you to this business is another key to your success. What was it that caught your eye? Products that were healthier, safer, or better than you could find in the retail stores? A medical condition that could not be fixed through traditional medicine but that was successfully treated through a network marketing product? The opportunity to own your own business without all the hassles of running a business all by yourself? Your prospects will be most interested in hearing about what you saw in this opportunity. Practice your story, use details that make it come alive, stick to the truth, and share it often.

And although it's important to tell your story, it's even more important to become a good listener. Listen to what others have to say. Learn from their comments. Adapt your presentation based on your customers' needs and concerns. The more genuine you are in your listening skills, the more successful you'll be in your presentations.

Day Fourteen: Teeth Are Best of All

LEARN TO TELL your story, become a good listener, and then hang on tight. Tenacity, determination, commitment, passion, and focus will become some of your greatest allies as you build your business. Stick with it. Sink your teeth into it. Don't let up. Hang on tight. Make sure they get your message—and take action.

Day Fifteen: Become a Great Networker

NETWORKING DONE WELL looks nothing like what most of us think of as networking. Forget about handing out great quantities of business cards or joining prospect-rich clubs or going out to "work the crowd." Instead become a real person who sincerely cares about others. Send thank you cards. Send birthday cards. Read the paper with your friends in mind—mail them relevant articles. Nurture friendships. Use the phone. Keep in touch. Help others connect with others. Be a resource. Make a contribution. Volunteer your time to worthwhile causes. Learn how to entertain. Share your friends. Share your knowledge and skills. Spend ten minutes each day doing something for someone outside of your family. Let your networks happen sincerely and naturally. John Kalench, one of the world's best network marketers, had the goal of creating a million friends in his lifetime. Imagine how such a goal would change your everyday approach. If you know how to give of yourself, you'll have the key to building a great network.

Day Sixteen: Get Rich Slow

THOUGH SOME may tell you otherwise, network marketing is not a get-rich-quick enterprise. It'll take time for you to build your organization. In fact, in the early months of your business, your hourly wage may be far less than what you're accustomed to earning. But remember this: This is a "get-rich-slow" opportunity. Those who stick with it, who invest time and energy into their business, will be generously rewarded down the line.

Network marketers talk a lot about "growing" their businesses. The metaphor is apt. What you put in the ground today might not look like much. But over time, with lots of care and attention, that tiny little sapling can turn into something magnificent. So keep your day job. Hold off on going full time until your income from network marketing is at least equal to your current salary.

Day Seventeen: The Golden Rule Rules

THE ONLY WAY you can possibly experience long-term success in network marketing is if you live by The Golden Rule. Treat others as you would like them to treat you. Think about what it means to provide good service. Pull out your pencil and start taking notes on the good and bad service you see. How attentive is the seller? What kinds of words is she using to talk about the product? Was she sensitive to your time? Did she express genuine interest in you? Did she seem competent? Would you come back to her again? If you can really zero in on the needs of your customers, and show how your product will meet those needs, you'll zero in on success.

Day Eighteen: Copy Off Your Neighbor's Paper

HERE WE GO AGAIN. First we tell you to practice The Golden Rule, and now we seem to be suggesting the opposite. You're right. In high school we were told to never look at our neighbor's paper, whereas in business we're encouraged to. Sam Walton said once that nearly all of his best ideas came from someone else's store. He spent one day a week going to other shopkeepers' stores looking for good ideas. Network marketers should do that too. Go to your sponsor's meetings. Go to a strong distributor's meeting. Learn however you can. One of the wonderful aspects of network marketing is that the normal competitiveness of the corporate world doesn't exist. In network marketing it is possible for all players to win.

And not all great network marketing ideas will come from within your own industry. Go, for example, to a Weight Watcher's meeting and try to figure out why this is one of the most successful self-improvement programs around. Look for ideas you can adapt for your own meetings: regularly scheduled weekly meetings, weekly measurement of progress, an inspirational/educational message, commitment in the form of weekly dues, and more.

Day Nineteen: The Box on Your Desk Is Your Future

MARGUERITE SUNG communicates with up to 200 distributors regularly. How does she do it? She uses the tools. Voicemail, e-mail, the telephone, snail mail, three-way calling, and more. Technology is giving network marketers wonderful tools that can link us with large, distant—even international—groups, all in a matter of minutes.

Companies are making it easy for you to build your own Web sites. And the corporate site becomes a tool for new customers to learn more about products and research and even order products. It's a new day. Those who not only use but celebrate these miraculous new forms of technology will be the winners.

Day Twenty: Be the Boss of You

CERTAINLY ONE OF THE freedoms of this business is that you don't have a boss with an alien agenda controlling the whats and whens of your life. But make no mistake about it: In this business you do have a boss, and that boss is you. You will need to be personally accountable for how you spend your time, for the results you produce, for the speed in which you produce them, for the consistency in which you work toward them, and for the style in which you produce them.

And one of the most stylish ways to produce results is to start with a plan. Each month write down what you hope to accomplish. Then break that apart with weekly accomplishments. The only way to accomplish a big job—and building a large network marketing organization is certainly that—is to take lots and lots of small steps toward your ultimate goal. Keep at it and before you know it that dreamed-about large organization is yours.

Another strategy is to hire a fictional boss. Who do you know who sets a high standard? Who inspires you? Your upline supervisor? A leader in another organization? Pick a person whom you admire and let her be your imaginary boss. Then at the end of each day have a short meeting with your boss. Literally! Review your progress toward goals. Did you do all the things you said you'd do? Did you avoid the temptation of procrastination and face your more difficult tasks with focus and commitment? Are you perfectly clear about what you'll need to accomplish tomorrow? Are you in line to meet your weekly, monthly, and yearly goals?

A word about time management: As a woman with a home-based business, you'll have many distractions. If you let them, your children and your chores can occupy your every waking moment. But it doesn't have to be that way. With a little time management, you can carve out the hours you need to build a successful organization. Turn the hours your kids are in school into your office hours. And don't let those hours slip. If your kids aren't yet in school, join or create a neighborhood child-care co-op. Hire someone to come help you clean your house. Two women working together for just two hours can clean just about any house. And as far as cooking goes, learn two or three totally simple meals that your family loves. Then on the busy days, you'll always have something good and simple to fix.

Day Twenty-One: Work with Matched Energies

AS YOU BEGIN to experience the benefits of having a network marketing business, a certain passion takes hold. You'll think of lots of women who need what you now have. The neighbor who works long hours in a job that seems to hold her back. Your friend down the street who needs but can't afford a new car. Your best buddy who's always dreamed of traveling to Europe. Just know that not all of them are ready to be rescued. It takes time for us to get to the place where we're ready to make changes in our lives. So as you prospect, give people the space to say "thanks, but no thanks." And instead, direct your efforts toward those who are responsive to your message, your new lifestyle, and your new business.

Day Twenty-Two: It's Easier to Give Birth Than to Raise the Dead

THIS ADVICE becomes important later in your career. As you begin to develop an organization, you'll have distributors who seem as if they should be larger or more successful than they currently are. You'll call them, encourage them, get commitments from them, but still nothing seems to happen.

While never giving up is great advice with some distributors, for others, moving on and finding someone who shares your passion may be your best strategy. Make a point to always bring new people into your business. This new life will invigorate you and your organization.

Day Twenty-Three: Imitate the Lucky

LOOK UP THE WORD "luck" in *Webster's Collegiate Dictionary* and you'll make an interesting discovery. Long ago, when the word was first given meaning, luck was simply "a force" that created good fortune. In other words, hard work could be the force. Tenacity could be the force. A positive attitude could be the force. Belief in self could be the force. Anything could be the force.

Only now do we think of luck as someone who's good by chance. In the world of network marketing, you will meet many who are considered "lucky." If you want to imitate their luckiness, you'll need to look more closely at their luck. What are they doing to create their own luck? Chances are they're making many more presentations than those who have less luck. Chances are they wake up each day expecting a certain amount of luck and so they dress for it, have thought about it, and are ready for it. Chances are they have a pretty polished one-minute presentation, five-minute presentation, and one-hour presentation. Chances are they have business cards in their wallets, product catalogs in their glove boxes, and a Web site on the Internet.

In other words, good luck happens to those who are prepared for it. So get ready for it and realize it.

Day Twenty-Four: Find the Diamonds in the Rough

WHEN YOU ASK the leaders of large organizations what's the most satisfying aspect about their business, the answer may surprise you. It's not the money, the status, the recognition, or the freedom. Rather, it's the tremendous pride they feel in watching others in their organization grow.

When Lili Willick was awarded the Watkins Year's Best Award, she recalls it as "one of the greatest moments in my life. But what topped that experience was having someone from my organization earn it the next year."

This business creates tremendous opportunities for growth. People from all walks of life, from all kinds of backgrounds, from all nationalities, have managed to build successful organizations. Learn to look beyond a person's current position in life and look for an inner spark, a positive way of interacting with people, an ability to follow through and you've probably found yourself a diamond in the rough.

Day Twenty-Five:
Be a Go-Giver

FOR A LOT OF US it's hard to imagine ourselves as "go-getters." But ask us to be a "go-giver," and suddenly we're up to the task. In network marketing giving of yourself is one of the best things you can do to ensure your success. Send thank you notes. Send lots of birthday cards. Jump in and help wash the dishes at a friend's party. If your friend is painting her kitchen, offer to help for half a day. Volunteer at your daughter's school. Have a ready supply of small, already wrapped gifts so you can commemorate life's little turning points.

Look for ways to say I care and I contribute. It'll be one of the smartest business moves you can make.

Day Twenty-Six: Realize the Power of Praise

KENNETH BLANCHARD'S and Spencer Johnson's hugely popular 106-page book, *The One-Minute Manager,* is based on three simple messages: set goals, give praise, and give reprimands. When such a simple message has the power to create an international bestseller that has sold more than seven million copies, you know the message is a good one.

If praise were a product, it'd be too expensive for most of us to enjoy it. Thankfully, this powerful fuel costs nothing. Because it makes a person feel good, those who get it naturally want to do more of what made them get it. It adds to the pride you feel about the work you're doing. And it creates loyalty between you and the giver. Praise is a major ingredient in any successful organization.

And one of the first companies to demonstrate its effectiveness was Mary Kay Inc. Started in 1963 by a woman who knew the power of praise and recognition, Mary Kay Inc. has become one of network marketing's great success stories. Though many elements (Mary Kay herself, exceptional skincare products, a balanced opportunity, an enormous market, and more) have contributed to the company's success, surely one of its most distinctive success qualities is the company's commitment to recognition. Those Mary Kay Cadillacs you see traveling down the road are a testimony to the power of praise and recognition.

Make praise a part of your everyday business style. And if you really want it to be felt—make it detailed and specific. Immediate praise is great. And if the effort was really significant, follow up with a mailed note or e-mail. Chances are the recipient will save that note and read and re-read it many times.

Praise is a powerful tool. Learn to use it, then use it as often as you can.

Day Twenty-Seven: Keep Things Moving

MOMENTUM IS A tremendous ally in this business. Always be on the lookout for ways to create and encourage momentum. Smart companies have developed "fast start" programs that allow new distributors access to special income pools if they meet certain qualifications within their first month of business. If your company has such a program, make sure you take advantage of it.

Initiate programs that get the group going: lunch for two at a special restaurant for the month's top producer, a silver star charm for all who reach a new status within the next three months, a homemade bookmark for those who are enrolling. The point is, keep their attention with meaningful recognition of their accomplishments. And once you get them going, keep them going with still more programs.

Day Twenty-Eight: Sharpen Your Saw

NO MATTER where you are in your career, don't allow yourself to be too busy cutting wood to take time to sharpen your saw. Go to meetings. Go to the annual conventions. Read books about the industry. Read books that have nothing to do with the industry. Subscribe to magazines. Talk to other people who are in sales within another industry. Take a class. Form a group with which to share and develop new ideas.

Make renewal a part of your everyday life, and you'll have more energy and more to offer others.

Day Twenty-Nine: Climb Over It!

THOUGH NEARLY EVERYONE can succeed in network marketing if they're willing to put in the time and effort, there is an obstacle course that all distributors must pass through en route to success. Your family will say no. A new recruit will need more encouragement than you have to give. A top distributor in your organization will tell you she's quitting so she can go back to school. You'll miss an important incentive program in spite of lots of hard work. These things *will* happen. And they have already happened to all who have gone before you.

When they happen, you need to connect not with the hurdle but rather with your goal that lies just beyond the hurdle. Look at the big picture. Pay more attention to the big benefits rather than the small obstacles.

Day Thirty: Be a Leader

MAKE NO MISTAKE about it, at the top of all large, successful network marketing organizations, you'll find a leader. This is a person who helps others achieve all they're capable of. This is a person with a passionate vision for the future and who encourages, coaches, and mentors others through that vision. This is a person who can establish and maintain successful relationships. They're active in their communities; they have strong family ties and many good friends.

It follows then that the single most important thing you can do in your business is to acquire and develop your personal brand of leadership. How will you inspire your organization? What habits have you acquired to nurture and encourage relationships? Are you helping others be all they can be?

Make a commitment to be a student of leadership. There are many articles and books written about the subject. Read them. Make notes. Talk to others, and ask them how they define leadership. Karen Hagen, a distributor from Watkins, tells others to "stand tall on the outside so they can stand tall on the inside." Write up a personal leadership statement and put it in your wallet. And take a minute every week or so to make sure that you're living up to this vision of leadership. The more emphasis you put on creating and developing leadership skills, the larger your organization will grow.

Month Two and Beyond: Repeat the Program

AS YOU NO DOUBT have come to realize, "30 Days' of Network Marketing Wisdom" is much more than a thirty-day plan. These morsels of wisdom offer up a lifetime of ideas and strategies for building your network marketing organization. Keep these ideas front and center as you build your business, and you'll learn about that business much faster. And come back again and again to these messages. The experiences you are about to have will give depth to the suggestions in the chapter.

Most of all, take a minute to relish the journey that lies ahead. You are about to take a giant step forward in your life. You'll meet new people and make new friends. You'll discover skills and talents you never knew you had. You will become a bigger person. Embrace it. Enjoy it. And share it abundantly with others!

PART TWO

Advantage:
Female

CHAPTER NINE

Meeting the Women

W HEN WE FIRST learned that the publishers had decided to call this book *The Very Best Opportunity for
Women: How to Get More Out of Life Through Network Marketing,* our first thoughts were, "Oh no!" For
starters, it smacked of hyperbole. Plus it was a mouthful that
people would never remember. And, we thought, it lacked
emotion and didn't speak to the female soul. But try as we
did to get them to consider an alternate, the publishers were
resolute: This was to be the title of the book.

So we busied ourselves with the sizeable task of writing
this book. And then something curious happened. The title
started to grow on us. The more we probed, the more we
compared the industry to the traditional business model,
and the more we learned, the less extravagant the title
sounded. This is, after all, an industry in which the inherent
female qualities of networking, intuition, compassion, nurturing, and sincerity are some of the biggest assets you can
have. This is, after all, the industry that has allowed many

women to become millionaires. Not only that, this is where mothers are finding balance, where female professionals and minorities are finding equity, where what sometimes is a limitation—being female—now becomes an advantage.

The stories you're about to read validate the title as well. Susan Waitley is certain that network marketing is the only place where a woman with no money, no college degree, and no prior business experience can earn a million dollars in just four years. Margaret Tanaka was a single mom and an Emmy Award–winning public television producer whose heart broke each time she left her child with the sitter and drove off to work. With network marketing she's earning a living and staying connected to her son, Luke.

Diane Chapman, an African–American, values the fair deal that network marketing gives to women and minorities. Robin Cohen leapt to network marketing because here she can experience geometric growth in her income, something unheard of in her former traditional sales job. Therese Razzante puts the flexibility of this business to the ultimate challenge: She's built a successful home-based business while raising six young sons. And Donna McDonald, a woman who was juggling a full-time job, a husband who traveled frequently, and small children who needed her care, saw network marketing as something that down the road would lighten her load without lowering her income.

The stories you're about to read do more than validate the book's title, however. These stories give readers a terrific chance to learn from those who have gone before them. These are exceptional women. They have years of network marketing experience and wisdom. They represent a wide range of network marketing companies. They come from all walks of life, from diverse backgrounds, and each shares her unique perspective on the business. To be around these women, to hear their stories, and to listen to their wisdom is to receive an incredible gift. It has been a priceless opportunity for us; we have learned many times over what passion and persistence can accomplish, and are better people for having spent time with these successful network marketers. If you're looking for a great upline sponsor, any one of these women would make an excellent choice.

Because we anticipate several questions you're likely to have about these women and their accomplishments, we offer our answers below, followed by solid evidence—their actual stories.

Q: Are they different from you and me?

Absolutely and no, not really. As you read the stories, you'll notice two things. Many of them did things that the rest of us might not have done. Yet all of what they did, each of us *could* do. Miki Crowl began her business by delivering catalogs in the dark before her kids woke up. Donna McDonald insisted that contractors working on her new house in a new city host The Pampered Chef kitchen shows. Grace Dulaney kept the faith while her business crumbled around her and because of it went on to greater heights.

Q: Did they all start with a bang?

Though some found success fairly quickly, others floundered. Nancy Jo Ryan, who now has The Pampered Chef's largest sales organization, started only because she wanted some Christmas money. Tami Fingerle wrestled for twelve months with the identity of her new profession. Kerry Buskirk meandered for seven years before she finally took the business seriously. Betty Miles' husband was dead set against her starting a network marketing business. (After conducting his own lengthy investigation, he not only agreed to her venture, he encouraged it.)

Q: **What's the truth about the income potential?**

Though there are a few exceptions, this is not a get-rich-quick business; rather it's a get-rich-slow business. Miki Crowl's first leadership check was $2.78. Betty Miles, who had an existing network from her insurance business, experienced rapid growth. After just four months in the business, she was earning $5,000 a month.

The women interviewed for this book have mature businesses. Nearly all of them needed at least a year before their businesses produced an income commensurate with their former salaries. And in three to four years, their incomes greatly surpassed the incomes they had previously received. Some of the women interviewed are earning $8,000 per month while others are earning in excess of $30,000 per month. (It should be noted that not all women interviewed divulged their incomes.) Each of the women interviewed is certain that her current income significantly exceeds what a traditional nine-to-five kind of job would, over time, have offered them. For example, Karen Hagen, who has only a high-school education, now earns an income nearly ten times what the corporate world would pay her.

Q: **Was a college degree a factor in their success?**

Absolutely not. Though all the women interviewed demonstrated great intelligence, having a college degree or even completing high school was not a factor in their success. Lili Willick, for example, completed the tenth grade in school, but feels she has a graduate degree in the school of life. Nancy Jo Ryan feels a college degree is sometimes a deterrent. Had she had a college education, she thinks she might never have considered this business.

Q: **What successful traits do these women share?**

Each reinforces the saying that successful people do what the unsuccessful don't. Though each of us *could* do what they do, we aren't always *willing* to do it. Beyond that, these women are willing to stick it out. As Diane Chapman says, "You have to stick and stay to get the pay." These are women who listen to their own inner voice and are able to ignore the nay-sayers and dream stealers.

Q: **What are the tough parts of this business?**

Nearly all of the women talked about learning to move beyond the word "no." They also talked about the importance of learning to meet people halfway. As Grace Dulaney says, "You have to learn to be responsible *to* your downline, but not *for* them. And you have to understand that often friends and family aren't the first to support your new venture."

Q: **How do they feel about the future of network marketing?**

There are many factors that are making network marketing even more attractive than it was only five years ago. The Internet is having a huge impact. Marguerite Sung has an international business with organizations in Taiwan, Japan, Europe, and Brazil. This wouldn't have been possible a few years ago. Also, the industry has a new kind of pride as it continues to attract women from all kinds of professional backgrounds. All these women see a bright future for network marketing and have every intention of being a part of it.

Q: **So how do you get started?**

Read all you can about the industry. Subscribe to the industry magazines. Move beyond the negative comments you may hear from family and friends. (Many women mentioned that some of their toughest customers were their closest friends.) Get comfortable with the word *no*. Do not take it personally. Have a vision statement written out and close at hand. Work your business every day. The hours may be flexible, but they're not optional. Network with others in the business who are successful. And always, keep a positive frame of mind.

Enjoy and celebrate the success of the women you're about to meet.

The Power of Belief

Courage Under Fire

Name: Margaret Tanaka

Home: Berkeley, California

Organization: Shaklee Corporation (nutritional products, personal care, water treatment systems, health and fitness products, and more)

Years in network marketing: 10

E-mail address: mlttanaka@aol.com

Web site: www.shaklee.com

Special achievements: Has built a successful Shaklee organization that allows her to work from home; be more available to her son, Luke; and volunteer for meaningful projects such as a Haitian food program.

IF YOU DIDN'T KNOW BETTER, you'd think Margaret Tanaka's business success came easily. She's friendly, attractive, bright, and well educated (graduated Phi Beta Kappa with a degree in communications from Penn State, plus earned a master's degree in journalism from the University of Wisconsin). In truth, Margaret's success was hard won. For three years she struggled with selling, she took "no" personally, and she didn't understand the industry. Then, in desperation she quit her job; committed to network marketing; and from that moment on, did not look back.

Margaret Tanaka knew it would be hard returning to work after her son was born. But she never imagined herself hunching over a dirty sink in a small office restroom pumping breast milk, stealing glances at her watch, and strategizing how to shoehorn a full-time workload into the three-day-a-week schedule to which her boss had agreed. A woman with a master's degree and a lifetime of success, she thought, shouldn't be living like this. "It took desperation for me to overcome my fears and commit to a Shaklee career," Margaret says.

Margaret had signed on with Shaklee three years earlier, but fear of rejection had kept her stalled in her business. "It was a sideline I had trouble committing to," she says, "but I also couldn't drop it because I knew in my heart it was right for me. The products were terrific, and the opportunities for a flexible, profitable business seemed limitless. But I just couldn't see myself in sales. My family had always worked in the helping professions—as ministers, teachers—and I thought selling meant forcing myself on people. In the early days I was so terrified of rejection I missed the most obvious opportunities.

"When I was pregnant with Luke, a woman in my prenatal exercise class said she hated her prenatal vitamins and asked for suggestions from the rest of us. I knew only too well how great Shaklee supplements were for pregnant women. Still, I lay there on the floor, speechless, afraid to admit that I was selling something. Talk about self-sabotage!"

Margaret can look back and laugh because now, seven years later, she's built a Shaklee organization that provides an income that approaches six figures a year for her family, plus she's helping many other women to do the same. "The key to my success," she says, "is when I came up with my vision: I saw a network of moms working together who wanted time for their children, who desired financial prosperity, and who also wanted to contribute to the beauty of the earth. When I began to see sales as service to others, all my fears dropped away."

Now, seven years later, she's built a Shaklee organization that provides an income that approaches six figures a year.

Was it that simple? Yes and no. That initial bolt of understanding had to be followed by research, positive thinking, and a more grounded sense of self. "One of the things I had to get clear on was the integrity of this industry. During my first years I heard some awful things about network marketing: people losing their farms or their life savings, destroying friendships, and more. I had to learn the whole truth about this industry. John Kalench's books (*Being the Best You Can Be in MLM* and *17 Secrets of Master Prospectors*) helped me, and so did *Upline* magazine. The amazing thing about this learning process is that the minute I knew how to respond to those stories, I no longer was asked about them.

"I also researched Shaklee's earth-friendly products, and the generous and fair sales plan, and understood that Shaklee is an ethical company that keeps me feeling proud and excited to be a business leader. Every woman—every person—

who is considering working for a network marketing company must check out the ethics of that company. Otherwise, how can you respect your business?

"Finally, I felt the connection between my heart and mind. In July 1993, I was still working that part-time day job, plus I had taken two evening jobs—custodial and data entry—when my husband, Rich, could be home with Luke. My attitude changed from despair to elation when I wrote down the day I was going to quit my job: January 31, 1994. I planned, you see, by then to reach the supervisor level, even though I'd only been taking home a small amount of money!"

"When I began to see sales as service to others, all my fears dropped away."

By September 1993 Margaret had reached the supervisor level, but hung in at her day job until the target January date. "There's a real power in knowing that your vision contributes to others. Suddenly, it wasn't just Luke and me, but the gift of giving other women time to be home with their children, and for all of us moms to use and sell environmentally friendly products. I found myself talking to other moms about Shaklee, and it felt easy. Because I had this larger vision, I stopped taking it personally when people said, 'No.' And more and more women were saying, 'Yes.'

"I started listening to personal development tapes and felt hope for the first time. I realized how out of control I'd felt earlier, like I had few choices or opportunities. I made myself believe that I had choices; I simply banished every negative thought from my head. I took to writing affirmations twice every day. It's important to use the present tense so that it feels real. I wrote: I am a Shaklee supervisor. I sell $3,000 in volume with ease. I attract business and business builders. I work with three motivated business builders. I radiate self-confidence. Not only did I write these messages down, I'd say them to the baby, to myself, because to change your business, you have to change your attitude. I knew that none of those opportunities would come true unless I got rid of my own fears and 'junk.' But it happened, and the business kept building once I committed to it."

Margaret's husband, Rich, was won over by her enthusiasm and business plan. Not only did he admire her vision of mothers having time with their children, but he wanted some of that time with Luke himself. Margaret's success with Shaklee allowed him the opportunity. In May 1994, Margaret's income was steady and sufficient enough for Rich to quit his full-time television job and become a freelance television technician. The joy of spending time with his son, Margaret's Shaklee income, and the flexibility of his own working hours enabled Rich, by 1997, to reduce his client base and work 25 percent of the time.

Margaret's income was steady and sufficient enough for Rich to quit his full-time television job and become a freelance television technician.

But it was a bittersweet blessing. On September 18, 1997, while attending a Shaklee party with Margaret, Rich experienced a fatal asthma attack. Although Rich had been diagnosed with asthma and always carried an inhaler, he'd never before had an attack severe enough to put him in the hospital. Tragedy struck the couple at a time of great happiness: the Shaklee business was solid, the couple had nurtured a large group of friends in Madison, Luke was a cheerful five-year-old, and Margaret and Rich hoped within a year or two to have another baby. Even with 911 emergency assistance, Rich, who was only thirty-six, couldn't be saved.

Suddenly Margaret, at thirty-four, was a widow. "My life turned upside down. I never expected this. Rich wasn't even sick! I was in such shock that I needed space for Luke and me to grieve and gather strength. I needed to take my son and travel, to see family members, to spend time by the water and in the mountains. Nature, family, and faith are what allowed us to regain our strength. And the women in my Shaklee organization supported me as I found my way through the healing process.

"I gathered my group together and explained what has become my philosophy about business and life. You know how geese fly in a V formation? The first goose is the windbreaker for the others, making it easier for the others to fly. I explained that I'd been that lead bird. Now I needed to fly in back for awhile, and have others take the lead. 'Give me a few months,' I said. 'Keep going and let me rest.' And of course they did. The group kept meeting and working toward their goals without me. And I was able to keep earning income the entire time."

Within a year Margaret returned, even more committed to the women who'd given her so much. With her television background, it was natural for her to start her own production company, Tanaka Productions, and provide personal growth tapes and videos for her organization. She began giving seminars, teaching others how to prosper personally and financially.

A year after Rich's death, Margaret made another life-changing decision. "I wanted to be close to my siblings," she says. "And Luke needed aunts and uncles and cousins nearby. We decided to move to California, and Shaklee made it easy. I didn't need to look for a job; I kept my organization going and am still as close as ever to the wonderful Shaklee

Margaret Tanaka's Network Marketing Wisdom

- *Be patient.* Everyone has her own timeline and lessons to learn. You can't want the business more for someone than they want it for themselves. If you talk to enough people, the ones who are ready will rise up.

- *Keep yourself motivated.* I'm a huge advocate for continual personal development work and lots of visualization of your goals fulfilled so that you keep yourself motivated.

- *Keep a positive attitude—no matter what.* Look for the gift in every experience. Every challenge offers opportunities to grow and learn.

people I've worked with in Madison and Chicago. Now I work three days a week—for five hours at a time—while Luke is in school. Once a month I send out my "A Message from Margaret" tape. I'm organized, and I get a lot done in a short amount of time.

"When I look back, I realize that my business only took off once I sought to serve other mothers and the earth. And it's the opportunity to serve others that's kept me going through good times and bad." So in the end, like her parents before her, Margaret *did* end up in a helping profession. Building a Shaklee business makes the world a better place.

Network Marketing's Passionate Professor

Name: Robin B. Cohen

Home: Yardley, Pennsylvania

Organization: Oxyfresh Worldwide, Inc. (air purification, dental hygiene, skincare, animal care, nutritional products, personal care, and more)

Years in network marketing: 7

E-mail address: rcohen6261@aol.com

Web site: www.oxyfreshww.com

Special achievements: Holds an appointed position on Oxyfresh's National Leadership Team overseeing field development. As a master director for Oxyfresh, Robin Cohen is a visionary of her own life. Not only is she building her own personal financial empire, Robin is teaching others to do the same. And the alarm clock that for so many years woke her each morning at 3:45 A.M. has been thrown away.

WHEN YOU LISTEN to Robin Cohen talk about network marketing, a chill runs down your spine. Her ideas, devotion, and simple way of communicating leave you longing to hear more. "The night I learned about network marketing," Robin says, "I couldn't sleep. Geometric growth, residual income, and helping others, which ultimately helps you, were hugely compelling concepts. From the moment I 'got' network marketing, I knew I could never again work in a tradi-

tional business model. For me, that first exposure
stant trigger for massive action."

Robin Cohen surely had what many would ha
ered a dream job. She was, after all, in demand, _____ly regarded, and taking home a six-figure income. Robin was selling seafood to area restaurants and hotels and working closely
with chefs, cooks, and restaurant owners. At her peak she was
selling roughly $7 million to $8 million in fish each year.

"My income was respectable," Robin says, "but I had to
wake each morning at 3:45 and sell under exceedingly pres-
sured conditions." Fish, as everyone knows, gets old fast;
and to sell the quantities she needed to sell, she had to make
at least 100 phone calls a day and
work a client list that included more
than 1,500 different restaurants and
hotels. The pressures of the job and
her work schedule were taking their
toll. She wasn't eating or sleeping
well, and she was becoming anemic.

> *"From the moment I 'got'
> network marketing, I knew
> I could never again work
> in a traditional business
> model."*

When Robin's general manager
realized that her results were good enough to put her salary
above his, her commission schedule was promptly reduced,
even though she had just earned a glowing performance
evaluation. "I felt undermined, and I knew I needed to find
another way. I experimented with a couple of network marketing companies, but there didn't seem to be a strong fit.
Then I went to an Oxyfresh Leadership Seminar, and I was
impressed." The quality of the people, the corporate infra-
structure, and the company's outside reputation all made
her feel that she'd found an organization that would work
for her.

Selling fish full time while trying to also work as an independent Oxyfresh distributor meant Robin was even more pressed for time. The moment Robin's Oxyfresh business produced its first I-can-survive-on-this check, she quit her work as a fish seller. "In truth, I left a little early. The early checks in this business can vary greatly. If I were to do the transition again, I would have held on until I had six months of a steady Oxyfresh income. That's when you can make your move safely."

But jumping early provided some important learning opportunities, lessons that would help shape her network marketing business. "When your vision is strong, you find a way. To supplement my network marketing income I organized a couple of garage sales. The first two I held I made roughly $2,600 each time. It was stuff I didn't need. It was stuff other people did need. And when neighbors and friends learned that I was having another garage sale, they came forward with lots of things for me to add to my sale. The world has a way of supporting strong visions."

Robin is certain that her business survived its early building phase simply because her vision was so strong. The key to a vision statement is to precisely define what you want your future to be and then write it down as if it's happening as you write. In other words, you put your ideal future into the present tense. "If you spend enough time reading, thinking about, and believing in that vision, it's as if it has already happened. My first vision statement revolved around freedom. My job as a fish seller made me feel like a caged animal. To be comfortable, I had to keep working. I couldn't live off of my savings. I had no financial freedom. My vision back then was to have a life where I didn't have an alarm clock. I wanted to be in a position of taking care of myself. And I wanted to partner with people who wanted to make amazing things happen."

In time, Robin was indeed part of a group of people who wanted to make those amazing things happen. "Network marketing is tribal. Not like a cult, but like a culture. We're a group of people with shared values who make big things happen. Recently, a friend of mine had a baby. She wanted guidance during those first few weeks, so she hired a new-baby nurse to come to her house to teach her what a new mother needs to know. Until only recently this was a job that mothers, aunts, sisters, or neighbors would have been responsible for. But today we hire a professional or take a class.

"We're a group of people with shared values who make big things happen."

"In network marketing, when you need support, you don't hire out, you simply ask within your group, and the person who can support you steps forward. We are each other's support team. For example, right now I'm hoping to partner with someone who understands computers and the Internet. I'm putting the word out, and very soon, the right person will come forward. I know that.

"This business demands that its leaders have positive energy. To make big things happen, you have to wake up with a positive attitude. And the way to do that is to literally flood your brain with positive messages." Robin encourages those in her organization to read uplifting books, listen to motivating tapes, and be wary of subtle, negative messages.

"One of the falsehoods of this business is that success can happen overnight. It doesn't happen that way. Because of the nature of the Oxyfresh product line, I work with a lot of dentists. Before a dentist can even begin practicing, he or

Robin Cohen's Network Marketing Wisdom

- *Use vision statements.* Imagine what you'd like your future to be. Write the script of your life. Don't put it in the future tense, but write it as though it's already happened. Then review your vision statement regularly. This was without question one of the most helpful tools I had when I was first building my business.

- *In the beginning, borrow from someone else's confidence.* Look into your upline for someone who's working the business the way you'd like to work yours. Then imitate their system and success.

- *Don't be a "salesperson."* People are brilliant about buying things. They don't need help in the buying; they need help in the understanding. Teach people about your products and let them "sell" themselves. Personally, I think of myself as a national educator for Oxyfresh.

- *Learn to let go.* Close down your adult daycare center. Though women are good at empowering others, we're not so good at letting go. You need to teach and train, but ultimately you have to let someone have his or her own spills and bumps.

- *As soon as you learn something, give it away.* Share what you know with others. Don't be a solo flyer.

she must spend four to six years learning the profession. Even after all that education, they're still just beginners; and it will take years before they're experts. Network marketing is really no different. It takes time, education, and practice to achieve in this business; you have to take a long view if you seek true financial freedom.

"Network marketing gives women the opportunity to teach and make extraordinary amounts of money that no other industry offers to everyone and anyone. There are no prejudices in our industry. No class, sex, color, or educational background will influence how well you do. The only thing that influences success is one's belief system. With every fiber in my body, I believe in network marketing. And those who know me know that about me. And soon they believe it for themselves."

Ain't No Mountain High Enough

Name: Diane Chapman

Home: Florence, South Carolina

Organization: Excel Communications, Inc. (long-distance service, paging service, Internet products)

Years in network marketing: 16

E-mail address: dianechapman@excelonline.com

Web site: www.excel.com

Special achievements: Diane is a member of Excel's "Top Performers Council"; member of Excel's Top 40 Income Earners; charter member of the Excel Eagle Team (leaders selected to help build the company during its first decade); selected as the year 2000 "Business Woman of the Year" for Florence, South Carolina. She is also blessed with a supportive spouse and son who help to keep her life in balance.

IF YOU LISTEN to the recorded message on Diane Chapman's answering machine, you'll get a hint why the community of Florence, South Carolina, selected her as the year 2000's "Business Woman of the Year." This woman's warmth, sincerity, and southern charm instantly draw you in. Born on a farm in South Carolina, the eighth of nine children, Diane has taken the brave and bold steps needed to move from good to better to best. Today she melds her friendly, people-loving personality with a massive dose of determination to lead one of Excel Communications' most successful sales organizations.

"I turn strangers into friends wherever I go," Diane says. "I was in a restaurant in Myrtle Beach, South Carolina, when I noticed the great skills our waitress used with her customers. I had a brief conversation with her about her work and suggested that she check out my Web site. When she contacted me later, I learned she was a single mother working two jobs to make ends meet. By day she was a nurse. By night she was a waitress. Now she's an Excel representative working toward the financial freedom and personal flexibility this business offers."

Diane Chapman's first job out of college was as a respiratory therapist at Richland Memorial Hospital and at the Veterans Administration Hospital in Columbia, South Carolina. Although she enjoyed working with the patients, she felt she was trading hours for money and that even with overtime she'd never earn enough to equal her effort and commitment. So when she first heard about network marketing through an insurance and investment company called Primerica Financial Services, she was instantly attracted to the idea of working toward financial freedom and helping others do the same. Soon she'd earned an insurance and investment license and was building a business of her own.

Although Diane enjoyed her work at Primerica, the biggest gift that she received from this experience was the chance to work with a man named John Lennon (no relation to the former Beatle!). Diane feels strongly that whatever success she has had in her life it is in some way connected to the lessons this influential man taught her. "Periodically he would handpick a group of financial advisors and take us on special trips showing us things we'd never seen before. We saw the beautiful homes of others in our business who were successful. We went on exclusive trips to New York City. Everything was always done in a first-class way. He got me to believe that great things could happen to me."

Then, as a way of saying thank you to one of Diane's significant clients, Diane agreed to attend an Excel meeting. Excel Communications is a billion-dollar network marketing company selling long-distance and other communications products. "This client had made a significant investment in my business; I felt I owed it to her to at least learn about hers. Though I wasn't thinking about moving to another company, I was impressed with what I learned. The idea that I could earn monthly income from my own long-distance service and teach others to do the same was very intriguing. I was also floored by the opportunity of future communication services that would be an additional source of residual income. Even though family, friends, my mentor, and my spouse thought I was making the wrong choice, I decided to split my time between Excel and my investment work. Pretty quickly, my Excel income eclipsed my income as a financial advisor. It was a tough choice to make, but I decided then to pursue Excel on a full-time basis."

That was in 1994. Since then, Diane's Excel track record has been impressive. Today Diane's monthly income from that source tops $20,000. She has more than 15,000 people in her organization and has helped dozens of families build significant and secure financial futures. Diane also serves on many of Excel's top leadership teams. "I knew I'd reached a new high in my career when Kenny Troutt, Excel's founder, asked me to join him and ten other leaders (all of whom where men!) on a flight from Los Angeles to Dallas in his privately chartered jet. The plane had an upstairs and a downstairs. There was a full bar and beautiful leather couches. My only thought was, 'If they could see me now!'"

Today Diane's monthly income from that source tops $20,000.

Although Diane has achieved much in her six-year Excel career, her success was neither instant nor easy. Each day she took the brave steps she needed to take to make her business grow. "In Florence, South Carolina, the Middleton family is the epitome of success. Since I've been a small child, I've always been in awe of that family. They owned Orangeburg, South Carolina's, Coldwell Banker business. Well, I decided I was going to present my business to Kenny Middleton. It was the scariest thing I've done. Needless to say, I took the presentation seriously and spent a lot of time preparing and practicing. I went in at 2:00 in the afternoon and didn't complete the presentation until 2:00 that night. And you know what? That one presentation, the most difficult one I've ever made, has had the biggest impact on my business. He not only became an Excel representative, he's brought many, many others with him into my business."

Diane also says, "Working in traditional businesses, there are many things that can keep you from reaching the top: race, gender, education, experience, and/or lack of connections. In network marketing there's only one thing to hold you back: lack of performance. In this business you're only known for your accomplishments. That corporation's computer only knows your ID number and your accomplishments. And that's enough to generate a check. Many people say network marketing is the first time they've been treated fairly.

"This business has been a blessing to me and my family. When my husband decided to change careers, my income gave him enough of a cushion so that he could look until he found the right thing. Today he's working eight to five for Wachovia Bank, and he's very happy. I'm also able to help my nieces and nephews as they struggle financially to get through college.

"To be successful, I've had to make sacrifices. But as a family we've found creative ways to make it all work."

"To be successful, I've had to make sacrifices. But as a family we've found creative ways to make it all work. We have weekly family meetings to make sure we are all on the same page. We discuss concerns, upcoming events, and more. Plus we have weekly prayer time. And when traveling, I make every effort to return home on an evening flight so that I'm here in the morning when my son heads off to school.

Diane Chapman's
Network Marketing Wisdom

- *If you have burning desire, you can succeed in this industry.* If you're an ordinary person with limited resources, yet you have extraordinary dreams and goals, this is the industry that can make it happen for you.

- *Don't mistake the beginning for the end.* The beginning is the tough part. But for those who "stick and stay until they get their pay," the rewards are substantial. Once you've built your sales organization, things change dramatically. Your workload lightens somewhat, you'll work within your comfort zone, and your income will exceed your efforts.

- *People don't care how much you know, until they know how much you care.* I have tried to master that philosophy for the last sixteen years. I believe in recognizing people and making them feel special.

- *Lead by example.* You can't ask others to do what you're not willing to do yourself.

- *Honesty is a powerful recruiting tool.* Women love the truth. Tell your prospects honestly about the effort this business requires; that way they'll come into the business with their eyes wide open and they'll be more likely to hang in there.

- *Focus on solutions and not on problems.* Those who succeed know how to step over their problems and get on to the solutions.

- *By the yard it's hard; but inch-by-inch, anything is a cinch.* Work your business each day. Consistency of effort is very important in this business. Keep at it, and soon you'll have created something substantial.

"And with a little creativity, a negative can become a positive. When I'm out late tending to Excel business, I want my son to know that I've come home even if he's already fallen asleep. I let him know I'm home by planting a big red lipstick kiss on his cheek. Of course, sometimes that means I have to put the lipstick on first. But knowing that when he wakes up he'll race to the mirror to check his cheek, it's an easy effort to make."

Diane Chapman eagerly and generously shares the benefits of her Excel business with others. She's a huge source of emotional and financial support to her nieces and nephews struggling to support themselves through college. She's a board member and an important fund-raiser for both the McLeod Regional Hospital and The American Heart Association. She's a frequent speaker in many of the community's local churches. She's a charter member, frequent speaker, and fund-raiser for the Jack and Jill of America organization, which helps young children learn new skills. And she's a lifetime member of the NAACP, often speaking about self-empowerment. Diane Chapman is a big believer in network marketing's first rule: To help yourself you must first help others.

The Power of Passion

What I've Done with Where I've Been

Name: Susan Elizabeth Waitley

Home: Rancho Sante Fe, California

Organization: USANA, Inc. (nutritional products, skin-care products, weight-management products, and more)

Years in network marketing: 5

E-mail address: swaitley@aol.com

Web site: www.usana.com

Special achievements: In just five years, Susan has qualified for the USANA Million Dollar Club (earning more than one million dollars in the past five years). She built residual income businesses for each of her seven children.

SUSAN WAITLEY had raised seven children and helped each of two husbands build highly successful careers. But when her second marriage ended, she had no real professional credentials of her own. Her high-school education, she knew only too well, would garner little more than minimum wage in the corporate world. Through network marketing, however, this high-spirited, fifty-four-year-old woman has work that she's absolutely passionate about. She's helping others find financial freedom through products that result in better health. And she's earning an income that stops you in your tracks.

Susan Waitley was married to the well-known life strategist Denis Waitley (best known for his "Psychology of Winning" tape series) when she first encountered USANA products. Through her husband's business, products of every variety were left at her front door. The big USANA box, like so many other boxes before it, was headed for the trash can when Susan felt a pang of guilt. To keep herself from feeling utterly wasteful and unappreciative, she reached in and grabbed one thing. It turned out to be the USANA Essentials—the supplemental nutrient powerhouse for which the company is best known.

Though spared from the dump, the packaged trio of supplements still sat on a shelf, unopened. But then she heard something on the news that opened her eyes to the value of taking supplements. She was heading out to the store to purchase some supplements when she spotted her stash of USANA products. She decided to use what she already had, so—for the first time in her life—she was taking a daily nutrient supplement.

For more than twenty years Susan has suffered from an inherited stomach condition called gastritis. Her symptoms were severe enough that at least once a year she was hospitalized for the condition. Though doctors told her that her stomach lining looked as if she'd swallowed battery acid, the medications the doctors prescribed didn't work, and their recommendations to avoid spicy foods and coffee were sometimes difficult for her to follow. After just a few weeks of taking the USANA supplements, a curious thing happened: Her symptoms disappeared. Could it be the supplements, she wondered? As a test, she stopped taking the supplements; the symptoms returned. Then she started taking them again; the symptoms disappeared. It was enough to make her a believer. Others must know of this discovery, she thought. And before long she was asking questions about the business.

"I saw this as something that was not only good for me, but good for others, too. I also started to think about building something for my children, an income that would supplement what they were trying to do professionally. I put each of the kids in my organization. Then I put my sister and my mother in my organization. My family members are now earning from $400 a month to $1,800 per week in residual income from the business.

"My family members are now earning from $400 a month to $1,800 per week in residual income from the business."

"The incredible thing was that I was being successful long before I really understood the compensation plan. I just kept talking to people, and success kept happening. I didn't understand that a slower build could create a stronger organization. I didn't understand that organizations are best when like-minded people are linked. I knew nothing, and still I was successful. How did I do it? I was passion on fire. And people

Susan Waitley's Network Marketing Wisdom

- *Passion and perseverance are what makes a person successful in this business.* You've got to feel something deep down, and you've got to want to share that with everyone you come into contact with. You also have to hang in there. Keep dropping the pennies in the jar, and before long you'll have something bigger than you ever thought possible.

- *Never prejudge.* People will always surprise you. The woman whose life seems so put together may desperately need what you have to offer.

- *Listen more than you talk.* Find out from people what their needs and desires are. In the beginning I spewed out all kinds of information about what I was doing. Now I know that was premature. When you first meet someone, find out about that person before you tell her about what you're doing.

- *Choose your company wisely.* Find out everything you can about the person who's running the company. In what other companies has he/she been involved? Integrity from the person at the top is critical.

- *Get yourself organized and set aside a certain number of hours per week.* This is a business that can be built from part-time effort. A slow and steady effort over time can offer dramatic results.

were coming from miles around to watch me burn. I didn't know about sales. I didn't know about marketing. I only knew that these products worked, and they could help a lot of people. So I talked to everyone I could about my important discovery.

I believe that women have a special talent for this business. We are natural caretakers. Our children, our homes, our husbands, our parents, and more. In this business, when you help someone else, you become successful. And helping others, whether with their health or with their financial situation, is without question the most rewarding part of my business.

"You know, something happened recently to me that I think is the perfect metaphor for the business of network marketing. I live in what is perhaps one of the most desirable and exclusive locales in the whole United States: Rancho Santa Fe. It's where the wealthiest of the wealthiest choose to live. You can only imagine the kinds of cars people from this area drive: BMWs, Range Rovers, Rolls Royces, Mercedes, Cadillacs, Lexuses, and more. Well, not too long ago I saw a woman dressed in coveralls whose car had broken down. Helplessly, she was trying to push the car out of the traffic. Those fancy cars simply honked their horns in frustration at the broken-down car. No one thought to stop and help her. I pulled my car over to the side of the road and held up my cellular phone. From across the road, I yelled, 'Can I help you?' I honestly believe that my network marketing business is just like that phone. My business is a help line for people who have needs, goals, and dreams, but no real way to fulfill them."

Where There's Crisis, There's Opportunity

Name: Lili Willick

Home: Saskatoon, Saskatchewan, Canada

Organization: Watkins Inc. (health/wellness, gourmet specialty foods, earth-friendly homecare products, and more)

Years in network marketing: 12

E-mail address: lili@point2.com

Web site: www.watkins-inc.com

Special achievements: Lili has a successful business that allows her to honor the other important aspects of her life. Along with others in her organization, she has been able to enjoy trips earned to places like Jamaica, Barbados, Banff, Spain, Bahamas, Portugal, and more! She has liberated herself from the "tied up, tied down" aspect of traditional business ownership, and no longer owns a pager. Now she is able to live with a "family first" priority.

MUCH OF Lili Willick's charm is that she's such an amazing bundle of contradictions. She's simply too smart to have only a tenth-grade education, too much fun to sound so much like an MBA, too cheerful to have struggled in life, and too young to be so wise. Lili Willick reminds us once again of another of network marketing's golden rules: *Never judge a book by its cover.* Fortunately, Lili's sponsor knew this rule when she first talked to Lili about the business.

Although Lili and her husband, Wendell, *appeared* successful, they were, in fact, touching bottom. Their Watkins business became their lifeline, rescuing them from debt, stress, pushed-back priorities, and a pager that went "eeep-eeep" in the night.

Lili Willick's career in network marketing, now more than a decade long, got started because of a diamond and sapphire ring. Really. Her upline sponsor was holding a special incentive: Any distributor who held a $1,000 Watkins party would be rewarded with this beautiful ring, a circle of precious stones. Lili, who had always loved jewelry but could never afford it, was determined to qualify. Though Lili gave it her all, she didn't quite reach the $1,000 mark for a single Watkins party. Wisely, her upline sponsor lowered the bar enough to reward Lili with the diamond and sapphire ring. It was an act that would begin a long and prosperous relationship with a woman who can move mountains if she thinks it's for a good reason.

Because of their workload, they kept sleeping bags in their office—which allowed them to work late into the night while their kids slept on the floor.

Lili and Wendell Willick surely didn't look like probable prospects. They had a booming carpet-cleaning and janitorial supply business. Lots of contracts, lots of employees, and lots of work. One of the contracts was with the owners of Saskatoon's largest office building. It was a job that paid $25,000 per month. "When the check arrived, for a day or two we felt flush," Lili says, "then we discovered that our payroll costs were $22,000. And that was before we paid ourselves!"

But money was only part of their woes. Because of their workload, they kept sleeping bags in their office—which allowed them to work late into the night while their kids slept on the floor. Unreliable employees were also a source of friction. Though they had many wonderful employees whom they'd gladly hire again, they also had those who chose to take naps in the closet, who failed to show up for their 1:00 A.M. shifts, and who wouldn't take responsibility for their work. And when there was a 1:00 A.M. no-show, Lili and Wendell were the only ones who could fill in. "The pager my husband wore," Lili says, "wasn't a link to our business; it was a tether!"

It was their experience with traditional business that made them most appreciate their network marketing business. With network marketing, they could have their own business without paying out for inventory and employees. The couple had no leases

They could take vacations when they wanted to, rather than worrying about all their employees' schedules.

draining their bank account because they worked from home. They could schedule the business around the family rather than have their kids plan their lives around the business. They could be home when the kids left for school and home when they returned. They could take vacations when they wanted to, rather than worrying about all their employees' schedules. Their earnings were equal to their efforts. And their team of sales associates were not employees, but in business for themselves as well, so their commitment level was often much higher. "To us," Lili says, "network marketing meant freedom!"

And although Lili and Wendell knew in their heads the advantages of network marketing, they still had to get beyond the hurdle well known to nearly all who have gone before them: "Will we have to really sell things?"

Lili Willick's
Network Marketing Wisdom

- *Remember that success in network marketing is attainable to everyone.* No matter what gender, race, level of education, or business experience you may or may not have, if you have the desire and are willing to "pay the price," you can succeed in this business.

- *Develop your potential strengths.* This minimizes your weaknesses and creates new, sky-is-the-limit possibilities.

- *Realize the power of your convictions.* Recognize how much power your own enthusiasm and belief can have in influencing others in your business.

- *Be a nurturer.* As women, we have the advantage of being natural "nurturers." This nurturing spirit will draw people to us. Plus our intuition helps us in understanding and evaluating other people's needs and values.

- *Plan and schedule.* When you're starting your business, build a schedule for yourself. Then talk to your family about your plans. Having their support will be key to your ability to stick to your schedule.

- *Remember that it's easier to give birth than to raise the dead.* One of the first lessons that a leader needs to learn is that you can't want for someone else; they have to want it for themselves.

Instead of using the hard-sell tactics, Lili operated on the principle that customers are most loyal when you make them happy. "Actually, it reminded me of my years as a waitress. I found that when I was friendly and gave the customers good service, they'd come back and ask to sit in my section. They became my regulars. It's the same with network marketing, which is why it's such a fun business. If you're a nice person who's interested in and likes people, your sincerity comes through. You're interacting with people, finding out what they need, and figuring out how to help them. Of course, you must be passionate about your products. If you don't absolutely love your products and use them yourself then you won't feel good when you make your sales and your sales success will not be as high.

"Four years ago my husband decided to start an Internet business of his own. Our network marketing income allowed him to follow a passion. And running our Watkins business on my own now has added to my self-confidence. My children are now old enough to understand what I'm doing and what I've accomplished. Jacquelyn is fifteen, Jordan is thirteen, and Colton is eleven. They see that Mom has prospered by her own hard work, and their respect for me has grown. That's one of the greatest gifts I've gotten from network marketing."

I Was a Home Party Snob!

Name: Tami Fingerle
Home: Churubusco, Indiana
Organization: Weekenders USA, Inc. (women's clothing)
Years in network marketing: 4
E-mail address: Tfing@aol.com
Web site: www.weekenders.com
Special achievements: Since she started her network marketing business, Tami's three kids (ages twelve, ten, and eight) are no longer in day care. In 1999 Tami and her husband enjoyed an eleven-day fantasy vacation in Fiji; Weekenders picked up the tab. Tami has work that she loves, customers she cares about, and fellow business builders who are her best friends.

FOR ELEVEN YEARS Tami Fingerle was a critical-care nurse specializing in cardiology at a major hospital. As a physician extender, she was second in command in terms of patient care, adjusting medication, educating patients, and responding to problems. It was work she loved doing. And it was work her parents took great pride in.

Then managed care arrived. The government and insurance companies gained more and more control of her industry, and nursing budgets became increasingly tight. Every minute of overtime had to be justified. She had more responsibilities and less compensation. "One day I realized forty years from now the people and institutions who were running my life would not know I had even existed. Bottom line: It's really your family that matters. Once I understood that, I knew I had to leave nursing."

Tami Fingerle had quit her nursing job just days before her frantic hair stylist begged her to model for an upcoming Weekenders fashion show. In all ways, Tami was a reluctant participant. Having just quit her job, she had no money to spend. Because Tami was a jeans and T-shirt kind of woman, initially she had trouble relating to the dressier look. She and the other models giggled about the matching poly-cotton knit clothes in the dressing room.

But Tami did get something from the presentation. She noticed that the other women attending enjoyed the clothes. And she noticed that the woman presenting the fash-

> *"One day I realized forty years from now the people and institutions who were running my life would not know I had even existed."*

ions seemed to be having fun. So before she left, Tami took the presenter's business card and made a note to call her the following day. Tami also remembered that while working as a nurse, a fellow admired nurse had quit nursing to pursue her Mary Kay business. The woman had gone on to earn a pink Cadillac and make sizeable gains in her income.

Luckily for Tami, her upline sponsor was someone to whom she could relate. Her sponsor was the same age as Tami, also had children, and was making money out of her home. "She was a beautiful, sweet person who was having fun at work. I wanted what she represented."

But how can a former critical-care nurse—someone who each day made important decisions about a vulnerable patient's care—change roles so completely and find peace in selling knit suits that weren't, after all, her style? "My first twelve months in the business were tough."

Her parents were embarrassed with her career switch. Her peers from the hospital were mortified. "What *are* you doing?" they asked. Her husband felt certain that the initial $1,000 investment would be less profitable than a trip to the Vegas casinos. And worst of all, Tami herself lacked faith in her most recent move. "Because we were broke at the time, my husband said, 'You must promise to pay this money back.' Though I assured him I would, inside I was full of doubts."

And it went downhill from there. For her first show Tami invited all the people she could think of who'd be likely to support her business. But by evening's end, her sales total was $49. She would have quit right then and there, but a Weekenders offer of three free demonstration items to starting coordinators who hold five shows in their first two weeks kept her going. Her next audience was the nurses with whom she'd once worked. "They at least showed some enthusiasm," Tami says.

Tami says she spent the next twelve months redefining what it meant to have a good job. As a nurse, although her contributions were great, her compensation was modest compared to her contribution. Though she was highly regarded, praise came infrequently. And though many thought her nursing job was ideal, she left home each morning with a sense of longing for her children.

As a critical-care nurse, Tami had become acutely aware of the income gap between nurses and doctors. The doctors could afford to take their families on lavish trips to foreign countries and give their families all kinds of luxuries, while Tami, earning a fraction of what the doctors earned, was always in poverty mode. And though the hospital she was working for was becoming more and more successful and her responsibilities were increasing, her benefits and compensation decreased.

Not being home with her kids was also troubling. "I left the house in the dark and came home in the dark. My daughter had repeated ear infections because she was exposed to so many sick kids in day care. And when I had to call in sick because a child of mine was sick, my absence was not always met with a sympathetic response."

Today, Tami says, there's no comparison. She feels as if she's living a whole new life. Finally, she's home with her children. Teachers and administrators at the school always know that they can call Tami when they need help. She frequently aids teachers in the classrooms and is there for the field trips. "I'm in control of my life, my schedule, and my destiny."

It's been four years since Tami signed her distributor application form. And still she's amazed that she's a Weekenders coordinator and that she's so completely happy with her new profession. "Every day, the incredible women that I work with in this business inspire me. Whenever I'm low there is someone else who is upbeat and there to lift me up. In this business, women are helping women. This business has also strengthened my relationship with my husband, who now jumps in to help and support me where he can. I truly believe that each woman I bring into this business can have everything and more than I have received from this business. What I do comes from the heart, and I think people can tell that and will follow that. I expect success from others because I know anything is possible. My beliefs and visions for other women allow them to

"I'm in control of my life, my schedule, and my destiny."

Tami Fingerle's
Network Marketing Wisdom

- *Women are really good at this business.* Women have such a great ability to talk and share with others. I believe that this is the best opportunity for women out there today.

- *Training is always important to your business.* Go to meetings, go to the conventions, go to the seminars. Stay fresh and make training an ongoing part of your business.

- *Start sponsoring as soon as you begin the business.* I often think of all the women I met early in my career who would have been wonderful in this business. They slipped through my fingers because I thought I wasn't ready to talk to them about the business.

- *Treat this business as you would any other job.* It is not a get-rich-quick scheme. It takes time, dedication, and belief to build a business. It doesn't happen overnight, and it will only happen if you are willing to work at it and do what it takes to succeed.

- *Ultimately you have to believe in what you're doing.* Some people have a belief right from the start; others need to see results before they can fully believe in the possibilities that this business offers. Look around you. Pay attention to those who have succeeded. Cultivate faith, and success is yours for the taking.

move forward so much quicker, especially if no one has ever given them that belief before."

One of Tami's most successful recruits now earns enough money so that her thirty-nine-year-old husband could retire and be at home with the kids. But when Tami first talked to this woman about this business, the woman thought Tami was nuts. Still, although she had a full-time job and a new baby too, she was willing to give it a try. Today she has one of Weekenders' largest organizations. And each and every day she gets to be home with her kids.

"When I left nursing and began a Weekenders business, I thought I had left the helping business behind. But I didn't. I'm helping women in different ways with this business. I'm helping them to feel better about themselves. I'm helping them find work that's more rewarding. I'm helping them get their kids out of day care. I'm helping them find more meaning in their lives."

The Power
of Commitment

One Hundred Opportunities
to Succeed

Name: Marguerite Sung

Home: Potomac, Maryland

Organization: Nu Skin, a division of Nu Skin Enterprises Inc. (face and body care, haircare, oral care, cosmetics, and more)

Years in network marketing: 12

E-mail address: marguerite@bigplanet.com

Web address: www.nuskin.com

Special achievements: Marguerite Sung has achieved Team Elite (highest level within Nu Skin) and is on the Blue Diamond Advisory Board. She has helped more than twenty people in her organization become millionaires. In the process of building their business, she and her husband are closer now, twenty-eight years into their marriage, than ever before.

MARGUERITE SUNG'S business not only turned her and her husband into millionaires; it caused the same transformation for more than twenty others who've joined her organization. So what's her magic? Pluck; simple, pure pluck—what the dictionary calls "courageous readiness to continue against unfavorable odds." Marguerite's early presentations were stressful and largely unsuccessful, but she kept trying. Her family and friends discouraged her, but she had made up her mind. She spoke no Japanese, yet she built an enormously successful organization in Japan. She had never lived in Hong Kong, yet now she has the company's largest organization there. And, although Marguerite was a female immigrant with a slight Chinese accent, her U.S. Nu Skin organization is one of the company's largest. Pluck and persistence are Marguerite Sung's magic.

For Marguerite Sung, her dream began with a house—a lovely house she saw in a golf-course development in Potomac, Maryland. It had big bedrooms, a big living room, and nice quiet surroundings. It also had a big mortgage. And although she was able to convince her husband that they needed this bigger, beautiful new house, she had another hurdle to contend with. "My challenge," Marguerite says, "was to find a way to pay for it."

Marguerite's son's karate instructor, Dr. Hung Tai Wang, had invited her repeatedly to hear about the Nu Skin products and opportunity. Each time she'd turned him down. Sometime between the third and fourth invitation, Marguerite saw a house that captured her heart, so she opened her mind to "an opportunity presentation." Marguerite remembers it well. "At that point," she recalls, "I knew I had to rethink my computer programmer job at a major international airline."

One of the first things Marguerite and her husband, Pat, noticed at Dr. Wang's Nu Skin presentation was that his hair looked a lot fuller and healthier than the hair of most men his age. He told them it was because of Nu Skin products. "Then he told us he was earning $2,400 a month, after only four months! That really caught our attention." Although Dr. Wang had a Ph.D. in physical chemistry and was clearly intellectually gifted, Marguerite and her husband could see that he was not a natural salesman. "My husband and I thought, 'If he can do it, we can do it!' Not that I expected to be successful right away," she adds.

After Marguerite signed up to be a distributor, she gave herself a goal of 100 presentations. "I figured it would take 100 presentations for me to go from being pretty awful to being a great success. Even if I was nervous at first, I'd get stronger with each presentation. That goal kept me from getting depressed in the beginning, when I wasn't very good. I kept plugging away, learning from my mistakes, and I did get better. My plan eventually worked."

Marguerite was willing to put in the hard work to realize her dream.

The next step for Marguerite was travel. Born in China, she had lived in Taiwan, France, and Taiwan again before coming to America as an energetic seventeen-year-old. "I was raised a traveler," says Marguerite. "When I worked at the airline, my whole family traveled internationally through employee discounts." But once she stopped working for the airline and devoted herself to Nu Skin, she didn't want to give up traveling. She was attracted to Nu Skin's status as an international business. She immediately saw global possibilities.

Marguerite was willing to put in the hard work to realize her dream. Although she no longer had friends or connections in Taiwan (she was, after all, in kindergarten when she left Taiwan the first time), she could build a business there. She met mothers from her son's Chinese language school in Maryland and got names of possible prospects in Taiwan. Armed with only a few names and a lot of optimism, Marguerite took off and traveled to Taiwan. Though her sons were still young, every six weeks she'd fly to Taiwan and spend two weeks building up the business there. She also has a huge group in Japan, although she does not speak Japanese. That's because early on she recruited a Japanese–American couple who saw the opportunity and ran with it.

"Network marketing helped all of my dreams come true."

Right now she's developing organizations in Europe and Brazil. "Can you imagine? I could never have had this life working for a corporation. Network marketing helped all of my dreams come true."

For Marguerite, one of the big positives about network marketing is the way it compares to the corporate world. Months into her first programmer job, she referred a newly graduated male applicant to the airline. He was subsequently hired at a salary higher than hers. "I went immediately to my boss, who carefully explained that *this* man had a family to support whereas I was single and had to support only myself. Back then that seemed like an acceptable explanation. Now I know better. We should all be earning according to our contribution," says Marguerite.

"In corporations, you're always competing against other people for the few good jobs. Of course, if you're a woman, you have to work even harder, and still the corporation can skip right over you. Even today, with so much competition for the best jobs, people are jealous of each other in corporations. Why should I be jealous of someone else who does a good job and gets promoted? With network marketing, there are no limits on the number of good positions. Strong people aren't a threat. The truth is, I want to recruit people who are even better than I, because they are more likely to become successful."

When Marguerite started working in 1970 after graduating from college, she was paid $5,000 per year. When she left her airline job in 1990, she was earning about $5,000 a month. That is, it took her twenty years to go from $5,000 a year to $5,000 a month. She started working with Nu Skin in September 1988, and by June 1990, her Nu Skin income was double her pay from the airline. In Nu Skin, Marguerite went from nothing to $10,000 a month in less than two years. "This," she says, "can only happen in network marketing.

In Nu Skin, Marguerite went from nothing to $10,000 a month in less than two years.

"Since we all succeed together, there's simply no competition and no stress in this kind of work. And for women, it's ideal because there's no glass ceiling. You can make incredible amounts of money with no one holding you back."

Marguerite feels that she was lucky because her husband, Pat, was supportive for many years. He helped the children with their schoolwork, and even demonstrated Nu Skin products to show the man's point of view. But still, he kept his full-time job. He agreed to join her when she met

Marguerite Sung's
Network Marketing Wisdom

- *Never, never give up.* The biggest reason for failure is that people quit too soon.

- *Follow up on opportunities.* Follow-up is very important in this business. New people don't yet realize the importance of following up and often miss out on some excellent opportunities.

- *Get over your fear of rejection.* If you were a waitress in a nice restaurant and offered coffee to your customers, would you cry if 50 percent of them said "no" to coffee? Of course not! The "no" in network marketing is really no different. It has nothing to do with your worth as a person. Also, when people are negative about network marketing, encourage them to investigate the industry.

- *Beware of dream stealers.* Some of our closest friends and loved ones were less than enthusiastic about our new business. Don't let their discouraging words alter your course.

- *Get yourself organized.* Talk to your husband about helping you with some of the household tasks. Cook meals in quantity and on weekends when you have more time. Freeze them for later.

- *Don't be afraid to recruit people who are more talented than you are.* In this business you don't have to be threatened by another person's talents. In network marketing, their success is your success.

- *Expect people to be negative about network marketing, but don't let their negativity deter you.* Some of my best recruits begin with a negative outlook on network marketing.

one condition: her Nu Skin *monthly* income exceeded his *yearly* salary. He was a senior attorney for a multinational oil company, and he never expected that his wife would indeed attain that from her network marketing business. But in October 1995, Marguerite's monthly income surpassed Pat's annual income. He resigned the following February. "It's been *our* business ever since," she says.

"In many families, husbands and wives grow apart because they're both so busy, and there's less and less in common between them. Our Nu Skin business has brought Pat and me closer together. But really, what happened to us I've seen happen to other couples who work together in network marketing. As one of my downlines says, 'After all these years of marriage, it feels like my husband and I are dating again. We've always loved each other, but now we're in love even more.' What could be better than that?"

And what about the house she worked so hard to get? "My parents live in it now, and Pat and I have built another house just down the street."

Pay It Forward

Name: Kerry Lynn Buskirk
Home: Augusta, Kansas
Organization: Mary Kay Inc. (cosmetics, skincare, fragrances, dietary supplements, and more)
Years in network marketing: 29
Web site: www.marykay.com

Special achievements: Has a career that still excites her after twenty-nine years. Has achieved the highest possible position in Mary Kay Inc.: national sales director. Has been included in the Mary Kay Circle of Excellence for fifteen years (sales in excess of $250,000 in a year). Travels regularly on Mary Kay incentive trips to such places as Tahiti, Monte Carlo, Italy, Greece, Bermuda, and London. Leads a balanced life of business, family, and faith.

IN 1972, WHEN Kerry Buskirk first became a Mary Kay consultant, she didn't quite fit the mold. She was nineteen years old, wore no makeup, lived in overalls, t-shirts, hiking boots, and a poncho. "I was a hippie without the drugs," she explains. Today she's a member of Mary Kay's $1 Million Club (the elite group of women who've earned more than one million dollars in commissions through Mary Kay Inc.) and is quickly approaching the $2 Million Club. And although this modest woman is quick to tell you that she's never done anything extraordinary in her career, you only need to know her for a short while to realize that doing the simplest of things with the heart, commitment, and persistence of Kerry Buskirk can in fact be quite extraordinary.

Kerry was working as a waitress at the Village Inn Pancake House in Tucson, Arizona, while her husband attended the University of Arizona. "It was a difficult period for us. We were newlyweds, no longer living near our families, having little time to spend together, and struggling to make ends meet," says Kerry.

Although Kerry and the other waitresses at the Village Inn were hardworking and loyal, the owners seemed to care too little for their employees and too much about the profits. One day, in frustration, Kerry walked up to the cashier and announced sarcastically that she was leaving her waitress job to go sell Tupperware. The cashier, who was already a part-time Mary Kay consultant, suggested that Kerry build a business with her instead. The department store job that Kerry had been considering to replace her waitress job paid only $2.50 an hour. With Mary Kay Inc., her friend said, she could earn more than $10 an hour. "Back then," Kerry says, "it was the lesser of two evils."

The department store job that Kerry had been considering to replace her waitress job paid only $2.50 an hour.

Kerry needed $250 (29 years ago) to start her Mary Kay business, and the only way she knew of to get that kind of money was through a bank loan. The young woman, dressed in jeans and hiking boots, walked into the bank and presented her business plan to the bank's loan officer. To her delight, he agreed to sign. His only stipulation was that they add another $50 to the loan; he felt sure she'd need some kind of dress to be successful in selling Mary Kay cosmetics. So with a bank loan and a rust-colored jumper (with yellow-yarn happy faces on each pocket), Kerry launched her Mary Kay business.

Just days into her new venture, Murz and Limon Malone, an elderly couple she'd regularly served at the restaurant, called to ask Kerry and her husband out for dinner. "We assumed it was because the Malones wanted to buy the painting my husband had displayed in the Pancake House," says Kerry. "Instead, they simply wanted to share some of their marriage wisdom: learn to enjoy football, have fun with each other, and try not to argue.

"But all I wanted to talk about," says Kerry, "was how I was going to change the world with Mary Kay." At the end of the meal, the couples said their good-byes, and the Malones went to their car. Kerry and her husband stayed a while longer in the restaurant. Minutes later Limon Malone came back into the restaurant with a piece of paper in his hand: It was a check for $300. "He said I was a different person today than I had been just days before and that if a Mary Kay business was the reason, then that business should be supported. He asked me not to return the money, but just to pass my good fortune on to others."

Though Kerry wanted to honor the generous gift by succeeding in her business, her success would be years in the making. "I always loved this business. But for the first seven years, I lacked the confidence I needed to work the business consistently. But then I set my sights on an incentive trip the company was offering. That experience taught me the value of mapping out a specific action plan and then working that plan consistently."

Once Kerry had discovered the power of planning, things started to happen in a big way. In Kerry's first twenty-one years in this business, she averaged $32,000 per year, a figure that includes her first seven years, which were marginal at best. If you average out her earnings for her whole twenty-nine years, her average shoots up to $68,000 per year. "Only in network marketing could a young girl without a college degree begin a lifelong career that would pay on average $68,000 per year."

If you average out her earnings for her whole twenty-nine years, her average shoots up to $68,000 per year.

Kerry Buskirk's
Network Marketing Wisdom

- *Don't trade what you want most for what you want right now.* Don't lose sight of your goals. Read them twice a day. Hang on to what you really want and try to work around what's getting in the way of what you really want.

- *Don't hope for big stuff from everyone you enroll.* In this business, a few people do a whole lot and a whole lot of people do just a little bit. And that's okay. One of my happiest consultants earns just $60 a month. She's happy earning just that much and happy not to have me pushing her into doing more.

- *To push forward, pull back.* Winston Churchill said that you couldn't push a string but you could pull it anywhere you wanted to. My goal is to draw people to me rather than to seek them out.

- *Timing is just as important in our business as it is in a comedian's.* Holding back is sometimes more effective than bursting forth. Give people a chance to get to know you.

- *Stay one more day.* The women who started SoHo pop continually thought of quitting. One was ready, but the other just kept saying, let's quit tomorrow. Very often we decide to quit just before it gets really good. Take it one day at a time and, if you're tempted to give up, try to hold off quitting until tomorrow.

"I think of my mother often when I want perspective on my career," says Kerry, whose mother has been a loyal and hardworking legal secretary for all of her professional life. She's loved her job and always made significant contributions to her boss's law practice. But now her mother's boss is closing his office, so Kerry's seventy-year-old mother will have to find another job to support herself. "Though she's devoted years to her profession, she does not have the nest egg I have with my Mary Kay business. In network marketing you build something that lives on."

Kerry attributes her success to qualities not often associated with network marketers. "Lighten up," she advises. "This business was meant to be fun and fulfilling. Try not to get fixated on your results; focus instead on your actions. And remember to approach people as you would like them to approach you. Ask lots of questions. Take your time; there's no race here. We'd all be more successful if we'd think more about drawing others to us rather than seeking others out."

Twenty-nine years ago, a generous couple gave a gift to a young woman who had little more than big dreams. Today, that big-hearted investment has proved its worth many, many times over. The yield on the $300 investment of confidence is not only evident in Kerry's success (income, travel, freedom, lifelong friendships), but it also lives on in the lives of the thousands of women who have joined Kerry's Mary Kay organization.

Bought Her Husband a Harley

Name: Donna McDonald

Home: Jasper, Georgia

Organization: The Pampered Chef, Ltd. (house- and kitchenware, cookware, and more)

Years in network marketing: 11

E-mail address: dmacpchef@aol.com

Web site: www.pamperedchef.com

Special achievements: In 1998, Donna reached The Pampered Chef's top management status, the title of senior executive director. (Of The Pampered Chef's 70,000 consultants, only fourteen have achieved this status.) Donna has earned the Top Performance Cluster eight times; these awards for the year's top achievers are among The Pampered Chef's most esteemed awards. Outside of her professional accomplishments, Donna has three sons who have personally witnessed how far self-discipline and self-motivation can take you. And her husband has learned to love the benefits of "subbing" for mom while Donna's holding a kitchen show.

ELEVEN YEARS AGO, when Donna McDonald made her first Pampered Chef presentation, her best friend worried that they'd have to call a paramedic. "I was so nervous, I was nauseated. But by the end of the night, I'd made $160, so I felt fairly compensated." Today, Donna McDonald has held more than a thousand Pampered Chef kitchen shows in kitchens all across the country. As one of The Pampered Chef's senior executive directors, she has achieved what only a dozen or so other women have accomplished. Donna says: "My success comes from the fact that from day one I've always loved my work at The Pampered Chef."

When Donna attended her first Pampered Chef kitchen show, she was a woman with a maxed-out schedule. "The last thing I was looking for was a part-time job. I had a full-time job as a meeting planner for a labor union. I had a husband who traveled a lot in his business, and I had two children under the age of two. And yet at that meeting, I saw opportunity: great products and a business that would tap my background in the hospitality industry. And if it turned out not to be the right business for me," Donna reasoned, "at least I'd have some great products."

> *When Donna attended her first Pampered Chef kitchen show, she was a woman with a maxed-out schedule.*

Today when Donna hears another woman say she's too busy to do the business, a little voice says, "sounds like an ideal prospect."

"I'm always on the lookout for women who are 'too busy.' These women have the most to gain from this business because in time it will lighten your load, increase your financial freedom, and give you time to do the things you want to do. Though I'm at the peak of my career, I have time for all my family commitments, and I'm able to ride my horse three times a week."

As Donna began her business, she discovered that she enjoyed more than just the products. Holding kitchen shows was a lot of fun. By turning her bite-sized bits of free time into business-building time, soon Donna had built up a part-time Pampered Chef business. And though she was emotionally ready to jump ship and leave her job at the labor union, she and her husband agreed that as soon as her Pampered Chef income equaled their $1,200 monthly mortgage, she could securely make the leap and work full time as a Pampered Chef consultant.

But just as her Pampered Chef business was gaining momentum, her husband was told that he'd soon be transferred from Chicago to Detroit, a city in which Donna knew not a soul. Though this might have stalled a lesser consultant, Donna didn't let the new location hold her back. "We were having a house built for us in Detroit. I simply told all the men who wanted to work on the house—plumbers, electricians, carpenters and more—that, before they could be hired, they'd have to have their wives or girlfriends hold a kitchen show. And it worked wonderfully!" On long weekends, while still working full time for the labor union, Donna would drive five hours to Detroit and hold four shows: one on Friday night, one on Saturday, and two on Sunday. "If I needed to," Donna adds, "I'd beef up the Hostess Program and offer the host a free baking stone."

What fueled this "double duty" effort was watching her income from her part-time job inch ever closer toward the income from her full-time job. By the time they were ready to make the move to Detroit, Donna's income had more than surpassed the $1,200 mark, and she had the go-ahead to begin working The Pampered Chef full time. "I often think about what moving to The Pampered Chef has meant to me and my family. Had I stayed as a meeting planner for the labor union, I would have been earning not much more than $23,000 a year. In 1998, just seven years into my Pampered Chef business, my income was $135,000.

"This business is built in small but daily steps. One of the great thrills I have in the business is watching the woman who arrives and tells me how much she dislikes cooking but then leaves having bought the most. The right tools can change your experience in the kitchen.

"This business has big highs and little highs and both are meaningful. The night I was recognized for earning a Performance Cluster in five categories (personal sales, recruiting, developing directors, first-line sales, and overall sales) was an absolute peak experience for me. There are also some small moments that are equally meaningful. I recently called one of my consultants. She wasn't home, but her husband recognized my voice. He said, 'I just want to thank you for the way you've believed in my wife. A lot of others would have walked away. You didn't, and it's made a difference.' It was one of the best things anyone has ever said to me."

Donna's boys have also benefited from Donna's home-based business.

Donna's entire family has shared in her success. Donna believes that because of her work with The Pampered Chef, her husband has had a chance to build a stronger relationship with their three sons. "Often he's the one who bathes our kids at night, reads them a story, and puts them to bed. My husband has said many times that this business has strengthened the bond between him and our sons." And Donna's boys have also benefited from Donna's home-based business. Not only have they traveled more often and to more distant locations—

Donna McDonald's
Network Marketing Wisdom

- *There's no "trick" to this business.* It's just a matter of putting your time in.

- *Your hours may be flexible in this business, but they aren't optional.* You can move them, but you can't re-move them.

- *Break your big goals down into daily size bites.* Big accomplishments are clusters of smaller ones.

- *Learn to love the telephone.* The telephone is the life-line to our business. I spend four hours minimum a day on the phone. My phone commitment is to return all calls within twenty-four hours.

- *Build from the heart.* If people see that you're enjoy-ing what you do, they'll gravitate toward the products and the opportunity.

- *As a new consultant, consider journaling your feel-ings.* These early experiences can be valuable to others you bring into the business.

- *Your desire will make you achieve your goals.* Your background, education, or past experiences will not reflect your future possibilities.

- *Become comfortable with the word "no."* Don't take it personally. Simply move on to the next person with a smile.

Australia, for example—they've also seen her business up close and have seen what self-discipline can accomplish.

When Donna and her husband recently celebrated their fifteen-year anniversary, Donna was able to give her husband the ultimate fantasy gift: a brand new 1999 Road King Classic Harley Davidson motorcycle. "My husband actually cried when he saw the gift. It was a wonderful experience for both of us."

The Power of Integrity

South Carolina's Biggest Little Capitalist

Name: Betty Miles

Home: Isle of Palms, South Carolina

Organization: Excel Communications, Inc. (long-distance service, paging service, Internet products)

Years in network marketing: 7

E-mail address: bmiles@myexcel.com

Web site: www.excel.com

Special achievements: Betty lives at the beach, enjoys quality time with her family, takes wonderful vacations, and drives a black Jaguar. She also has the money to share with those less fortunate and will soon travel on a small mission to Moldova (a small country near Romania and Russia). She used her Excel business to pay off a $300,000 debt. As a senior director at Excel, Betty and her husband are members of several achievement-based Excel groups: Top Performers, Top 40, and the Million Dollar Masters Group (those who have earned $1 million though their Excel business).

TO SHOW THE VIDEO of the Betty Miles story you'd need a remote control. You'd start by fast-forwarding to the end: the part where the 5'1" Betty Miles is being introduced by the governor of the state of South Carolina as the state's biggest little capitalist. Then you'd rewind to the beginning: the part where Betty's first husband has professed his unfaithfulness and is asking for a divorce while Betty's mother is reminding her daughter of her responsibilities to her three great sons. You'd then jump to the middle: the part where Betty's current husband, who happens to be South Carolina's secretary of state, is saying to his wife, "*Don't even think about starting a network marketing business.*" Then back to the end with a long list of credits rolling and the orchestra playing triumphantly.

Betty Miles is being introduced by the governor of the state of South Carolina as the state's biggest little capitalist.

In law school, the insurance business, and love, Betty Miles bumped heads against the old-school male mindset. In 1965–1966, as a law student at University of North Carolina at Chapel Hill, she was one of three women in her class of 200. Betty says her fellow male students distrusted the motives of their female classmates. "They were convinced we were just looking for husbands," she says. After her first year of law school, Betty married her fiancé, whom she'd met in college, and became a full-time wife.

Later when Betty took a commissioned job with a large insurance company, the owners of the company felt that all corporate deals should go to the men, while the women should focus on selling to teachers and nurses.

Before long Betty realized that to make any real money she'd have to start her own brokerage firm. And although she was very successful in the industry, she always had to struggle. Once she made a presentation to the corporate board of directors for a major bank. She showed them how to fund a lucrative deferred compensation plan while also generating several million dollars' worth of tax savings for the bank. It was an awesome plan and the board members loved it. But the sixty-five-year-old chairman said, "Little lady, we love your numbers, but we want to see your boss." Betty's first impulse was to tell them that *she was the boss*, but then she devised what she thought might be a more acceptable plan. She went back to her office, arranged for another male insurance agent to attend the next meeting with her, and split the large commission with him—*just because he was a man!*

Still later, her first husband, after twenty-six years of marriage, decided he needed his space. Though Betty encouraged him to consider counseling, he explained that for years he'd had one foot out the door, and now he was determined to depart completely. Betty was devastated. She lost weight, cried constantly, and kept asking herself what she could have done differently. Her pastor said that she had a choice to make: She could be bitter or she could get better. "Believe me," Betty says, "better is better!"

Though she couldn't have known it at the time, all these experiences were priming her for a deeper appreciation for network marketing. Even so, by all accounts, Betty did not have the "likely prospect profile."

"For starters," Betty says, "I wasn't desperate. I had a successful insurance business and was earning $100,000 per year." The even greater limitation was that her second husband, a politician, did not want his wife to start a network marketing business. But like so many others before him, Betty's husband would soon realize that the common misperception of network marketing is different from the reality.

In 1993 Betty and her husband Jim were lucky enough to live next door to Steve and Kathy Newton. Steve was head basketball coach at the University of South Carolina, and Kathy was a science teacher. As both couples had the entrepreneurial spirit, they often talked about different kinds of business ventures, from buying a car wash to opening a pizza parlor. After attending a coaches' meeting in Kentucky, Steve came back talking about a new telecommunications business, suggesting that Betty and his wife Kathy work the business together. But when they began watching the Excel presentation video, Betty's husband, Jim, realized that Excel was a network marketing company. He made it clear that he did not want Betty to participate in any way with this kind of company.

Betty, on the other hand, saw possibilities. Her work with her insurance business made her more appreciative of the kind of business Excel was. No employees. No overhead. And a tiny up-front investment. She also knew that the insurance industry was making drastic changes. Many companies were selling policies directly to the public, bypassing the agents, via television ads and the Internet. And all of that would mean that soon she'd be working harder and earning less.

When Betty began to understand the Excel offering, that she would be giving people the opportunity to start independent businesses that required no inventory, no deliveries to make, no money to collect from the customers, and no complicated material or paperwork, she said, "Yes!"

Though Betty was eager to begin her business, she floundered a bit and did many things wrong. But through it all, her enthusiasm was contagious and spread quickly. "I absolutely loved every minute of it." And the more she shared the business with others, the more she saw it changing lives for the better. "I was able to convince people that they could succeed too. I think I convinced them because I truly believed it myself. I honestly believe anyone—regardless of age, sex, race, or education—can make network marketing work if they're willing to pay the price, to keep trying and never quit."

> *She floundered a bit and did many things wrong. But through it all, her enthusiasm was contagious and spread quickly.*

Though Betty feels she has a gift for this kind of business, she also knows that it took her many difficult months before she realized her gift. "I spent my first nine months in this business as a coward. I wouldn't shut down my brokerage company, and I only worked the network marketing business part time." In that short period of time, though, her income reached the same level as her insurance income. She was so surprised that she decided to split her time fifty-fifty between her "real" job and her network marketing business. "At nine months my monthly income had reached $17,000, and I knew that I had to go full time."

Betty Miles'
Network Marketing Wisdom

- *To be successful you have to be willing to do the things that unsuccessful people refuse to do.* Work hard, care about others, and motivate them to join you on your new path.

- *Women have a natural talent for the business.* I honestly believe that women do this business better. Women have the ability to make people feel good, to make people care, to make people want to help others. And that's the real secret of this business.

- *Earn what you deserve.* One of the key benefits of the industry is that you're paid what you're worth and treated the way you deserve to be treated.

- *Network marketing is one of the few businesses you can start up and become independently wealthy without making a big financial investment.*

- *Look for people who care about changing their lives.* These are the kinds of people who will be motivated to succeed in this business.

- *Make use of the Internet.* With the Internet we have a link to the world. Ten years ago you could not have done network marketing the way we can do it now. We absolutely can talk to anybody in the world.

- *Remember that this business is not a hobby or a social club.* Those who are good at the business always treat it like a business. They read a lot about the industry. They attend seminars and training meetings. They are dedicated to their success.

- *Cultivate friendships.* The friends you make, the life-long friends, are the best things about this business.

Betty's monthly check has gone up from there. Today Betty Miles has one of Excel's largest sales organizations with more than 14,000 people just in her first seven levels. She has personally helped thousands find the kind of freedom and flexibility that she's found through her Excel business. Today Betty's energies are attached not to earning more but rather to helping more and more women discover the self-confidence that comes from knowing how to financially support themselves and their families.

And how did Betty finally convince her husband that network marketing was a reputable business and worthy of her time and effort? First of all, she softened his stand against network marketing by earning a lot of money. Intrigued, he decided to initiate a substantial investigation of the industry. His twenty-five-page report affirmed not only the legitimacy of network marketing but also Betty's complete passion for it.

Service Before Self

Name: Therese Razzante
Home: Highland Heights, Ohio
Organization: The Longaberger Company
Years in network marketing: 13
E-mail address: btrazz@aol.com
Web site: www.longaberger.com
Special achievements: Therese is able to be home
    for her family and still has the personal satisfac-

tion of being a successful businesswoman. She, her husband, and their six sons worked as a team to qualify for an all-expenses-paid trip to Disneyland. Therese's regional sales team includes 230 consultants in twenty-two states. And though she has enormous responsibilities at home, she still manages to keep her personal sales levels high.

THERE ARE DETAILS about a person that *suggest* who they are. Then there are details that *declare* who they are. Being the mother of six boys is a declaration. But being the mother of six boys while operating a hugely successful home-based business is as defining as anything could possibly be. Therese Razzante's toddlers sit in on her branch meetings. Her older sons chart her progress toward her business goals. She has Christmas organized before Thanksgiving. She has a special "while-I'm-on-the-phone" toy basket. She has a special "things-I-can-do-while-waiting" basket that she grabs when for some reason she's in a holding pattern. She uses the "I Spy" game to get her house cleaned ("I spy something that needs to be picked up"). Hers is a business built during her children's naps, between loads of laundry, and while running errands. Therese Razzante is living proof that when your priorities are straight, when you know how to delegate, and when you keep a positive attitude, you can do virtually anything you set your mind to.

It was Therese's husband who first saw the potential of a Longaberger business. Therese had agreed to host a show, and her husband decided to sit in too. He liked what he saw and was certain his wife had the skills to duplicate what this consultant was doing. After the show, Therese's husband asked the consultant how much she made and learned that in those three hours she earned $125. He was then certain that entering this business would be a good idea.

"My husband pulled me aside and said I should try this business," Therese says. "He saw the extra income. I saw the fun of having my own business."

At the time Therese first hosted a show, she and her husband both had jobs at Deepwood Center, the Lake County Board of Mental Retardation. Therese had been a direct care worker for mentally retarded adults for four years and then had transferred to the school and worked as a teacher's assistant for three years. She has an older brother who was born developmentally challenged so special education had been her field of choice.

> "My husband pulled me aside and said I should try this business."

Therese loved her work at Deepwood. She enjoyed working with the individuals, organizing outings and activities, and being involved in goal setting and annual plans for her caseload. She learned sign language and worked closely with a three-year-old autistic girl at the school. "I had a wonderful opportunity to work in a very rewarding environment," says Therese.

Therese sees similarities between her work with Longaberger and her work at Deepwood. "I organize meetings, write newsletters, plan and organize bus trips to The Homestead and Dresden, Ohio (our company headquarters). The most enjoyable part is just like my previous job; I can help others set goals and help them achieve their goals. Today in my Longaberger business I have six branch managers and seven management-bound associates on my management team. These are people who have built substantial businesses through Longaberger, and I have enjoyed helping them achieve this."

Without question, the greatest benefit Therese sees in her Longaberger business is that it allows her to be both a successful business person and a successful mom. Therese's priority is her kids. "I have the opportunity to work my schedule to attend all my boys' sporting and school events, and do other activities with them because I can set my own work schedule. I'm here to help them with their homework or to ask them how their day went as they come off the school bus. I'm mom to them. Yet they've also learned a lot about business simply from watching me."

One of the keys to Therese's success is the wonderful partnership she and her husband have created. They met in high school, when he was class president and she was spirit coordinator. While in high school Therese was awarded the school's "Service before Self" award. After high school they worked together at Deepwood Center. In fact, Therese's husband was so successful at bringing others to Therese's business that he decided to create a business of his own. Today he's a branch advisor with Longaberger.

Therese's business could not have succeeded without enormous support from her family. "I have been fortunate that my husband, early on, was able to see the 'big potential' with my business. Many times he flexed his work schedule to allow me to attend training meetings, all the while enjoying the opportunity to spend more time with the children." Therese's husband not only offers emotional support; he enables the business by doing some paperwork and other tasks.

Whether in business or at home, Therese has learned that to succeed you have to ask for the support of others. "I delegate jobs to my consultants when I'm planning meetings. If I ask for volunteers and don't get any, I delegate. And I do the same with my sons." For example, she has a son who likes to stack and build, so she has him unload the dishwasher. She writes down jobs on pieces of paper and lets her sons choose the ones they want to do. If they wind up with a job they don't like, they can trade it with another brother. "I know the talents of my family and my group, and I pull on their strengths. I appreciate anyone who helps me out in any area of my home, family, or business!"

Therese also credits her success to the lessons her parents taught her. Therese was the ninth of twelve kids. "My parents always put the needs of their kids before their own needs." Therese's mother, who has since died, was supportive of her business from the very beginning. Today Therese still feels her mother's generous heart is a part of her business.

"Network marketing is by far the only business that you can meet wonderful people and build relationships that will last for years."

"Network marketing is by far the only business that you can meet wonderful people and build relationships that will last for years. I have an extended family of hundreds of wonderful people throughout the United States, all because of my Longaberger business. I bet I could get stranded in any one of our states and find a Longaberger friend to help me out!

"And one day in the not-too-distant future, I'll have six daughters-in-law. You can be sure that I'll do what I can to bring them into this business!"

Therese Razzante's
Network Marketing Wisdom

- *Commit to success.* Determination, persistence, and a positive attitude all play a part in the success of a network marketing business.

- *Recognize the opportunity that network marketing provides.* My brother is a very successful accountant and businessman. He was president of a company before he turned forty. In his view, he's amazed that I was able to start a business of this magnitude with an investment of only $385. He is most impressed with the way I've leveraged that small investment into a sizeable, profitable business.

- *Work at your business daily, be persistent, and do not give up!* This is not a get-rich-quick, sit-back-and-watch-it-grow type of business. Success will come through years of hard work, determination, and a positive attitude.

- *Look at the big picture.* Ask yourself what you are doing that will make a difference next week, a year from now, or five years from now.

- *Don't let the little things hold you back.* Worrying is a time waster. I believe that something good can always come from situations that look bad.

- *Make a daily to-do list and be sure to do the most important stuff first.*

Helping Others Succeed

Name: Miki Crowl

Home: Ottumwa, Iowa

Organization: Avon (cosmetics, skincare, decorative accessories, fragrances, giftware, and more)

Years in network marketing: 15 (Nine years as a corporate, salaried employee, and six years as an Avon representative)

E-mail address: avonmiki1@hotmail.com

Web site: www.avon.com

Special achievements: Miki has finally found a lucrative career that allows her to put her family commitments before all others. She has two daughters in private colleges, something she never could have done if she hadn't started her own Avon business. Through her Avon business, Miki has traveled to Hong Kong, Puerto Rico, Cancun, and many cities in the United States. She was ranked in the top five in her region (nineteen states) in leadership in the last six years. Miki has earned the Spirit of Avon Award (given to those who best represent Avon's values and dedication to excellence).

AS A DISTRICT MANAGER working for Avon corporate, Miki Crowl had the ideal vantage point for comparing the low-risk corporate life to the rough-and-tumble life as an Avon rep. On the corporate side, she had secure salary and good benefits. As an Avon rep, she'd start from ground zero with no benefits and an income that would take time to grow. The flexible hours, though, would give her time for family commitments. In 1994, after nine years of watching others make amazing things happen, Miki Crowl jumped the Avon corporate ship to become a representative. And she's never looked back. Today she's earning more than twice what she would have had she stayed in the salaried position. Her business allows her to hold true to her "family first" values. And incredibly, she feels the best is yet to come.

When Miki Crowl hears the words, "Let me talk it over with my husband," she cringes because she too has said them. And when she did quit her corporate job to start selling, she also "talked it over with her first husband," and all he could say was, "You'll never make any money." Miki heard those words so many times that she finally relented and gave up selling.

But much has changed since then. Her unsupportive first husband has been replaced with a very supportive second husband—and today she has a thriving Avon business. Her

Today she's earning more than twice what she would have had she stayed in the salaried position.

income is inching toward the six-figure mark. She has 730 people in her sales organization. And she's helped thirty-three other women build successful Avon network marketing businesses, as she did.

After leaving work on the corporate side as a district manager, armed with a new husband, Miki was ready to be successful. This time she knew what to expect. She'd talked her decision over with her new husband and her kids. And they all understood that for a while, things would be tight. When her first product order was only $78, she wasn't discouraged. When her first leadership check was only $2.78, she still wasn't discouraged. She knew enough to know that in this business, those who stick it out are always the winners—even when their rewards are small to begin with.

And bit by bit she began to build her business. Before the kids would wake she'd be out in the neighborhood delivering Avon catalogs. Attached to each catalog was a personal note. And she always followed up with a phone call. "I firmly believe that follow-up is one of the most important parts of this business. If we wait for our customers to call us, we will be like the Maytag repairman—very lonely!"

Another tool that's been useful in Miki's business is classified ads. Her approach couldn't be simpler. The ad simply says, "Avon Reps Urgently Needed," along with a number to call. Miki feels successful if the ad brings in four to five new recruits. "You'll meet with someone who responded to the ad, and they'll look and sound absolutely perfect. They say all the right things. But then nothing will happen. And then you can meet with someone who looks like nothing much will happen, and before the week's over she's called in a huge order. This business has taught me never to prejudge. The world is full of wonderful surprises."

> "This business has taught me never to prejudge. The world is full of wonderful surprises."

Now, one of the up-and-coming "wonderful surprises" in Miki's business is a woman who's willing to work hard for her dreams. Several years ago, this woman started a home-based daycare business so she could earn money and also have more time with her kids. But the reality just wasn't what she imagined. The owner of a daycare center just doesn't have a lot of time to give personalized attention, not

Miki Crowl's
Network Marketing Wisdom

- *Don't be afraid to turn good customers into recruits.* Yes, you might lose some of your retail business, but in the long run, building recruits will mean more to your business in terms of residual income.

- *Build deep into your organization.* Don't let your first line or personal recruits get all of your attention. You'll have a stronger organization and more secure income if you build deep and support your second and third levels.

- *Focus your energy into helping others succeed.* Let all other considerations come behind the goal of helping others succeed. If this is your mission, you will succeed.

- *Make sure that what you do is something others can duplicate.* For example, if you want to motivate someone, think of something that others can duplicate. Although an expensive gift might be motivating, it's not something that your newer people can afford to offer. Public praise or a heartfelt note is something anyone can duplicate.

- *Work harder, and you'll get luckier.* Hard work creates "luck," so focus on working hard and your luck is sure to improve.

even if some of the kids are her own. So now she has set her sights on duplicating Miki's success. By day she works her daycare business, and by night she works her Avon business, sometimes scheduling as many as four or five appointments a week. Just as soon as her Avon income equals her daycare income, she'll begin working Avon full time. "She is exactly the kind of person I look for in this business. She's organized, she's a hard worker, and she sees what can happen down the road," says Miki.

"This business has given me so much, as well. I have financial freedom that I could never have achieved through a traditional job. My daughters are both in private colleges and that wouldn't have been possible without my Avon income. My self-confidence has grown enormously. I know I can do just about anything I set my mind to do. My husband has new respect for me and the things I've accomplished through this business. He's become one of my biggest supporters. And my kids understand what rewards can come your way if you work hard and don't give up."

The Power of Leadership

Leading with Grace

Name: Grace Dulaney

Home: Escondido, California

Organization: Big Planet, a division of Nu Skin enterprises (communications and integrated technology products)

Years in network marketing: 10

E-mail address: graced@bigplanet.com

Web site: www.bigplanet.com

Special achievements: Professionally Grace distinguished herself by becoming the first presidential director in Big Planet, as well as a Blue Diamond in Nu Skin (Nu Skin's highest level of success). All of this, she accomplished as a single mother of two, working the business part time. Grace is now married to one of her first-level executives.

Today they are expectant parents; Grace will be both an at-home mother and a financial contributor to the family through a flexible leveraged business.

IF YOU WERE climbing a mountain with a group of women, and you found yourself at the halfway mark questioning your ability to continue on to the top, you'd be wise to slip in behind someone like Grace Dulaney. There's just something about Grace that tells you she'd have the grit, skills, and talent to take it to the top. Grace was only two weeks into her Nu Skin business when she announced to each of her six upline executives that she was going to be a Blue Diamond, Nu Skin's highest level of achievement. Today Grace is both a Blue Diamond and a presidential director. Many women and men have also climbed to the top simply by following in her sure and steady footsteps.

When Grace Dulaney heard her first Nu Skin presentation, she was so immediately intrigued by the message that she was actually imagining herself in front of the room giving her own presentation. "I was so 'ready' that my third month with Nu Skin I created more than $30,000 in volume and became an executive. The daycare business I was running back then limited my free time, but I was committed. I made phone calls while the kids napped. And my business began to explode!"

Grace was born and raised in San Diego and attended three years of college at the University of California, San Diego and the University of California at Los Angeles. After having spent two summers in Europe during college, her travels had fueled her desire to get out in the wide world and work. She left college, then spent the next fifteen years beating herself up for that decision. "As someone who does not quit anything and also values education, I saw this as a failure. I kept telling myself, 'I'll never have a real job because I don't have a degree.' Of course once I discovered network marketing, I realized that I'd never *want* a 'real job.'"

Grace's dream in college was to own an international business. Imagining that a job with a travel agency would allow for international travel, she became a travel agent. "For eight years I sat behind a desk and sent everyone else traveling. I remember thinking as I sat at that desk, 'If someone would just walk through that door and show me a business, I could do it.'

"After my divorce I realized I was paying half my salary to daycare so that someone else could raise my kids. So in 1986 I started a daycare business that I ran from my home. I spent about

"My third month with Nu Skin I created more than $30,000 in volume and became an executive."

$4,000 converting my garage to a classroom, getting licensed, getting supplies, etc. I never advertised. I just filled up due to word of mouth. For four and a half years, I was my own boss, made a respectable income, and was home for my kids."

But she was missing out on other things. During the first four years, she worked nonstop and never took a vacation. When she finally took a vacation to Australia, she learned what traditional business owners know about vacations: *When you're not working, you're not earning.* While she was off spending money in Australia, her business was closed, and no money was coming in. Financially, she took a hit.

"On my flight home I had two revelations. Having your income tied directly to your own efforts becomes a noose around your neck. My long-lost dream of having an international business simply had to be resurrected. Somewhere over Hawaii, I became determined to find a way to do business between the United States and Australia.

"Three months later I was invited to look at Nu Skin. The company was operating in the United States and had just opened in Canada. They were planning on launching into Australia, Europe, Asia, and so on. This grabbed my attention. And the concept of leverage was explained to me. Having just experienced no leverage on that Australia trip, it made sense, and I knew this was the business for me.

"Then I toured the corporate facilities. There were about 400 people at a conference hosted by my upline. I was shocked by all the men in their Wall Street suits. The caliber of professional people in the business blew me away, and I knew then that I'd found my niche. My business was off to a fast start."

But then tragedy struck. Grace's father, age sixty-two, died from cancer. Three months later her twenty-five-year-old brother died in a motorcycle accident. Six months after that Nu Skin was put through intense media and regulatory scrutiny, and she lost all but one of her downline executives and several of her upline executives. She had just closed her daycare to go full time, so this chain of events was devastating. She lost her car, her house, her downline, her upline, and two more family members (little nephews, two and six years old, in a car accident). "There were mornings that I wanted to say, 'Go away, harsh world!' However, *hope* sustained me!"

Throughout the immense changes, Grace never lost faith in the company and the opportunity in her hands. Soon the company was again moving forward, opening new international markets, and launching a new division. "As long as the company's here . . . I'm here," was Grace's firm attitude. "I did whatever it took to stay in the business and not give up on my dream. I did marketing for a dental lab owned by one of my downlines; I worked in a retail clothing store, and unbeknownst to *anyone* else (including my family), I even cleaned houses to make ends meet—all of this while also building my Nu Skin business. I established a very large group in Mexico and traveled to Europe to open those markets."

When Grace's seventh-grade son wanted to attend a private military academy, she created a position for herself as director of marketing/recruiting for the school. With his tuition covered and a steady income, she could devote more time to her Nu Skin business. She also made some great contacts through the school for her network marketing business. At this point Nu Skin was focused on Thailand and the Philippines.

As part of her life's mission to help others, Grace started a nonprofit organization that supported adoption as a choice for unwed mothers and supported programs that encouraged teen parents to create healthy beginnings for their babies by continuing their own education. She helped create a phenomenal mentoring program for teens and hosted six major fundraising events in a year and a half, including a huge Christmas party with the San Diego Chargers.

She set ambitious goals and moved quickly toward the goal she'd set more than seven years earlier of becoming a Blue Diamond. "The huge success of the nonprofit organization and the recruiting and leadership skills I developed in my role as founder/chairman of the board gave me great confidence in my network marketing business. I walked—floated—across the stage to receive my Blue Diamond award."

Soon Nu Skin would unveil the newest division of the company, Big Planet. "This is where I saw my future. I saw a window of opportunity to move into this and go for the top leadership position, presidential director." Grace spent

Grace Dulaney's
Network Marketing Wisdom

- *Commit to your goals.* If you summed up the one message of all self-help books, that message would be: Commit to what you want to do, and be willing to do whatever it takes to get there.

- *Self-discipline equals self-love.* Develop a daily habit for success that sets you up to win each and every day.

- *Instill hope in those whom you enroll, yet always paint a realistic picture.* You are responsible *to* your downline, not *for* them.

- *Don't burn bridges . . .* protect your circle of influence, for they are your greatest resource for building your business.

- *Utilize your warm circle of influence to lead you to the right people.* The real "juice" in this business lies between your warm market and the cold market. Remember that six degrees of separation connects you to everyone.

- *You can only control what you do.* You can't control what your upline or your downline does, or what the company or world economies do. When you really understand that one, you'll have learned a big lesson.

three months positioning and became a presidential director six days before the company was officially unveiled. She recruited seventeen new first-level executives in ninety days and in the first three months her group created over $100,000 in volume.

"Today I'm happily remarried with a new baby on the way. I have a strong business that allows me to enjoy a recurring leveraged income that is no longer dependent on my efforts alone. I love the work I do. And for the first time, I'll have a business and a baby that I can tend to from home. Big Planet is my palette from which to paint, my stage on which to dance. It's the vehicle that allows me to fully express my purpose in life, which is to enrich lives with abundant gifts of passion, awareness, and divinely inspired grace."

She recruited seventeen new first-level executives in ninety days and in the first three months her group created over $100,000 in volume.

Uncovering the Magic

Name: Karen Hagen
Home: Abbotsford, British Columbia, Canada
Organization: Watkins Inc. (health/wellness, gourmet specialty foods, earth-friendly homecare products, and more)
Years in network marketing: 13
E-mail address: karen_hagen@telus.net
Web site: www.watkins-inc.com

> **Special achievements:** Part of the Executive Group, the highest level at Watkins Inc. Has earned fourteen world-class trips during her network marketing career.

WHAT ARE THE CHANCES that a woman re-entering the workforce at forty, with only a high-school diploma and a bit of secretarial experience, can make it to the top using no more than her natural talents? Excellent, Karen Hagen would say—if she chooses network marketing. Asked what she likes best about her business, Karen says, "There's no ceiling on my income, or the level I might reach!"

Karen Hagen began working as a secretary right out of high school. By the time she moved to Seattle at age twenty-two, she knew her own capabilities. When a recruiter told her she should be at least twenty-eight years old to apply for a position with a top executive in a big firm, she wasn't willing to listen. "Just let me try," she said at the interview. "I know I can do this job." She was hired and worked as the secretary to the vice president, and was not yet twenty-eight years old when she quit to start her family.

Three children and thirteen years later, she was still enjoying being a full-time mother. However, it was all too clear that they needed a second income to maintain their comfortable lifestyle. Reluctantly, she agreed to go back to work. She found a part-time secretarial job.

The business world had changed while she'd been gone. No more Royal typewriters on the desks; everyone had a computer. She had to learn new skills. That didn't stop her; she managed so well that, before she knew it, she was working full time.

Her children were still young, her husband was often away, and it was nearly impossible to keep up and cover school holidays and summer vacations. The money wasn't very good, either. Worse, she noticed that women around her, who had been in the business a decade or two, still didn't have either good pay or serious responsibilities. Why work so hard in a job with no future?

She quit to work in her husband's business. There, she thought, at least she'd be able to come and go as she pleased. Wrong. "As owners, we were always 'first in, last out,'" she says.

She fell into network marketing almost by accident. She had bought Watkins products, liked them, and was looking for a way to buy them

She fell into network marketing almost by accident.

wholesale. She didn't even understand that the recruiter was offering her a business opportunity. Finally, she agreed to become a distributor and see what it was all about. Her husband teased her about her "cute little business." Not for long, though.

As she got acquainted with the organization, Karen noticed that the other Watkins representatives she met, mostly older men, were missing some major opportunities to expand their businesses. They were focused on products, not people. They weren't building the customer relationships that assure repeat purchases. They weren't networking. They weren't thinking about ways to help the consultants working for them, or new ways to help themselves.

"There's a better way to do this," Karen thought. She began phasing out of her husband's business to develop some of her ideas for her own "little business." Trying to visualize what she wanted to accomplish, Karen looked for models within the Watkins organization and didn't see anyone who was where she wanted to be. Instead, she found a mentor outside the organization, a friend who was a successful corporate executive. Having a mentor helped her learn management and leadership skills and to build her confidence.

Karen did something no one else she knew was doing; she gave parties to show and sell her products, and to recruit new representatives. Working two evenings a week, she discovered, she could make as much as in a forty-hour-a-week job. She asked other women to host the parties, and then invited them to accept distributorships. If the hosts weren't interested, other women who attended the parties often were. Soon she had a number of women working in her organization.

One of Karen's management secrets, though, is that she never thinks of her consultants as working "under" her. She treats them as partners. "This is about affirming yourself, helping others, and capturing the momentum," she says, when she talks with her consultants. She stresses that she is not trying to cultivate followers; she is cultivating leadership.

> *"There's magic within people, if you can uncover it—especially in women."*

"This is not about competition, either. You have to move over so that someone else can move up."

Karen believes in giving lots of verbal recognition, encourages her consultants to visualize themselves as successful and dress the part, believes in standing by people, but not in "hand-holding." As she puts it, "People want to know they did it themselves."

She also believes in potential and tries to nurture confidence and natural talents. "There's magic within people, if you can uncover it—especially in women," she says.

Karen Hagen's Network Marketing Wisdom

- *Make it a family enterprise.* When Karen went back to work, her children were eleven, fourteen, and sixteen. Network marketing gave her the freedom to be involved in their activities. She also involved them in her business. They helped her unpack orders, stamp catalogs, and even sell products to their teachers and friends' mothers. Today, all three children are involved in sales and marketing. Karen believes that seeing her become successful in business helped them develop self-confidence.

- *Take advantage of the network marketing lifestyle.* Asked about network marketing versus a conventional job, Karen listed these advantages in capital letters:

  Opportunities to travel

  Time with the family

  Free time, and the money to have fun in it

  Freedom to live anywhere in North America and take the business along

  Retirement lifestyle without waiting for retirement age

  The security of residual income after retirement

- *Make it through the tough times.* Here are Karen's hints for making it through:

  Stay focused on doing business and helping others.

  Don't get caught up in the "small stuff."

  If it can be fixed, fix it; if it can't be fixed, move around and past it.

  Keep your belief and spirit strong.

  Choose a few special people to talk to when times are tough.

After thirteen years in the business, Karen is one of the most successful Watkins representatives in Canada. She can make more in a month than a good secretary does in a year. Several years ago, her husband quit joking about her business and joined it. They work together well because they divide responsibilities on the basis of their strengths and because he shares her philosophy about growing the business. "I'm not selling vanilla," he says, "I'm selling the opportunity to sell vanilla."

That Royal typewriter has been left in the dust; Karen has established an interactive Web site to keep in touch and share ideas with the women who work with her. Problems? "I'm a bit of a perfectionist," she admits. "Sometimes things don't get done the way I'd like them to. But I try to stand back. People support what they help create."

An added benefit of Karen's business has been to make her children confident of their own abilities and the possibility of succeeding as entrepreneurs. Recently Karen's daughter, who is now doing well in her own sales business, asked her mother for some words of wisdom. "Just act like a duck," Karen said, "all calm above the surface, but paddling like crazy underneath."

Probably Karen's energy and work ethic would have made her successful in any career. The blessing is that, reentering the workforce at age forty, she found a way to exercise her considerable management and leadership skills without ever having to worry about pumping up her resume, buttering up the boss, or bumping her head on a glass ceiling. Network marketing let her uncover her own magic.

Business by the Numbers

Name: Nancy Jo Ryan

Home: Orland Park, Illinois

Organization: The Pampered Chef, Ltd. (house- and kitchenware, cookware, and more)

Years in network marketing: 14

E-mail address: Toolsforsuccess@aol.com

Special achievements: Transformed a part-time, "money-for-the-holidays" business into The Pampered Chef's single largest sales organization. Loves each day of her business whether it's holding a show or helping others realize their dreams. Has taken twenty-one expense-paid incentive vacations to worldwide destinations. And still is able to be a room mom, a field trip chaperon, and help with the car pool.

NANCY JO RYAN loves numbers, and numbers love Nancy Jo Ryan. Although it's been fourteen years since she signed on as The Pampered Chef's 190th consultant, she can tell you without pause how many shows she had in Month One and what she earned: ten shows and $582.73. "To do this," she says, "I worked two hours at my desk and eight hours outside my home per week. In my first month of business, I earned $14.57 an hour." Today, almost 700 shows later with a party average of $844, Nancy Jo Ryan lives with some of the very best numbers in this industry. She is responsible for leading more than 100 people in her first line and has developed The Pampered Chef's largest overall organization, with annual sales in excess of $25 million. She has more than 1,800 men and women in her organization. Her income went to six figures in her fifth year and hasn't slowed since then. These numbers have earned Nancy Jo twenty-one Circle of Honor Awards from The Pampered Chef as well as the esteemed Legacy Award.

Though Nancy Jo Ryan is a celebrity among Pampered Chef consultants and her kitchen show has been featured on CNN, to her neighbors she'd rather be known simply as Nancy Jo, the woman next door. Until a few years ago this humble approach was working: No one in the neighborhood knew she was anything more than the neighbor who happened to be a Pampered Chef consultant. But when a neighbor chanced to meet another Pampered Chef consultant, the story was out: Nancy Jo Ryan, the woman next door, is Numero Uno for The Pampered Chef, a $600-million-dollar company. Nancy Jo, the woman next door, has a home-based business that's a model to Pampered Chef's 60,000 other consultants. Her style, her system, and her success are closely watched. Her income is the stuff of legend.

> *Her income went to six figures in her fifth year and hasn't slowed since then.*

Although Nancy Jo's achievements have an otherworldly quality, her view of herself is completely grounded. *Nancy Jo Ryan is the girl next door.* She attributes her success to basic qualities that almost anyone can cultivate: determination, commitment, and enthusiasm. Her formula is practically mathematical: Make a plan, pray about it, then work the plan.

Nancy Jo Ryan knew that she loved numbers when she was just sixteen years old. That's when she held her first accounting job. By the time she was twenty, she was managing a twenty-five-person accounting department for a large manufacturing firm. "I was young, but I knew my stuff. I already had four years of professional accounting experience. And though I didn't 'technically' have a degree in accounting, I had completed every single college-level accounting course there was to take. The firm hired me immediately and 'loved' my references."

Although she loved her work, her fifty-hour work weeks became unmanageable once she was married and expecting her first child. She and her husband chose instead to live conservatively, forgoing vacations and other extravagances so that she could be an at-home mom. But by the time her second child was eleven months old, after more than seven years out of the workplace, Nancy began to feel an urge to get out of the house and take a part-time job. Making a little Christmas money was her goal. Predictably, the quantitative Nancy Jo was specific about her requirements: no more than two nights a week, at least $10 an hour, no weekend work, Wednesdays off, the month of December off, and no child-care costs. "Your boss is going to love you," was her husband's comment.

Two weeks later, on a friend's recommendation, she began her Pampered Chef business. Things went well. She loved the work. She went 50 percent over her hourly wage expectations, and she was able to take most of December off. And after only two-and-a-half months of work, she had fifty people on a waiting list wanting to host Pampered Chef kitchen shows. Nancy Jo is proud to say that, from the beginning, she never asked for hosts—they simply came forward requesting to host shows, with their friends and family.

Nancy Jo took the holidays off, but by mid-January she decided to resume her business. In February, she hired five people and by April she was a director. "I was loving every

Nancy Jo Ryan's
Network Marketing Wisdom

- *Make a plan. Work the plan.* Sometimes when a consultant is off track we go back to the reasons she started and look to the numbers. Most often those two elements will reveal where the consultant has gone astray.

- *Learn to embrace the journey rather than focusing solely on the destination.* What's been key to my success is my sincere love of helping people. Loving what you do each step of the way is my model for success.

- *Give joyously to others.* The connection between giving and receiving is most apparent in this business. If you give wholeheartedly to others, what you get back will far exceed your expectations. That's how to build a business.

- *Remember, network marketing can be like riding a roller coaster with many highs and lows.* Whatever you do, don't quit too soon.

- *FAYC: Forget About Yourself Completely.* Worrying about yourself is not productive in this business. Focus on others and your business will grow.

minute of it," she says. During Nancy Jo's first year in the business she earned $14,700. In her second year she earned $26,500, working about twenty-five hours a week. In her third year she earned $49,700 and worked about thirty hours a week. In her fourth year she worked thirty-five hours a week and earned $97,500.

"In a way, I break the rules of direct selling. My primary goal isn't only to sell, it's to have fun too. I tell my guests that if there isn't anything they need they should feel completely free not to order. I tell them, 'It's okay to simply enjoy the food and the fun.' Perhaps that explains why Nancy Jo has never asked a guest to host a show. Those who attend have the kind of fun that deserves to be repeated.

Even though Nancy Jo Ryan heads The Pampered Chef's largest sales organization and has an income commensurate with her achievements and responsibilities, it's not this aspect of her success that she's proudest of. "Three years before I started my Pampered Chef business, I prayed for a ministry with women. I never dreamed I would find this ministry *through business*. Like everyone else, I have had my share of life's struggles. But the Lord has shown me how to find my way out of difficulties. Those life lessons are of great value and have allowed me to encourage others in their lives and businesses as well."

"My primary goal isn't only to sell, it's to have fun too."

Very often in this business, what makes you weak makes you strong. "For much of my life, I felt limited by not having gotten a full college education. Now that I have a Pampered Chef business, I actually have *thanked* my parents for not sending me to college. If they had, I may never have found network marketing and The Pampered Chef."

Afterword _____

THE COOPERATIVE SPIRIT of women, both as individuals and in groups, has made this book possible. To help our readers continue their quest toward a full-time career or even a part-time opportunity in network marketing, we want to share the resources and tips submitted to us from others in the industry and to give recognition to those who have been part of this collective endeavor.

The appendices that follow provide you with a variety of tools for further research, broken down by sub-categories so that you may refer to them as needed. The wisdom shared by those already walking this path is super, and we are confident you will find their information useful along your journey.

How to Contact the Authors

Feel free to contact the authors by e-mail:

Angela Moore: angelam@ida.net
Lisa Stringfellow: simpletruths@yahoo.com

Appendix 1: Tips and Wisdom from Women in the Industry _____

W HAT FOLLOWS IS a collection of tips and wisdom from women (and a few men) in the industry. Individual quotes are attributed to the contributor. Other tips that were similar or given to us by more than one individual are combined and paraphrased to be more helpful to the reader. (A list of contributors whose input was the basis for this collective advice can be found in appendix 3.) These tips are divided for easy reference into six categories: recruiting, women helping women, maintaining balance in your life, choosing a company, what it takes, and general business tips.

Recruiting Approaches and Tips

"Be organized! Keep information to the point—don't overwhelm people with too much information at one time." —Ellen Weber

"Be direct but soft. Pull back to push forward, not seeming too eager." —Kerry Lynn Buskirk

"Start with some good ole female bonding! Then really ask powerful questions that lead to the heart of your prospect, unleashing the emotions that are going to move her into action." —Grace Dulaney

"I believe in touching the heart of a woman. It's not overnight success. You must have self-discipline. It is a numbers game. You need to love people. See the people, see the people, see the people! Be patient—Rome was not built in a day." —Carolyn A. Ward

"Use three-way calling." —Deborah Coronado

"I have two small children. I take them to the park playground and spend the first thirty minutes just listening to women complain about husbands being gone, getting into trouble about spending too much money, not enough money for lessons, sports, or whatever. Then I show them how, with Excel, they can change all of that." —Regina Fisher

"Never turn down an opportunity to meet people. Learn from successful people. Be prepared to do business [to prospect] at all times." —Lorry Davis

"Smile, speak from your heart, and listen with your heart." —Jeanne L. Wendt

"Honesty! Be honest with women about all aspects of our business—the flexibility to work around your kids, but also the fact that you will have distractions you need to work through." —Barbara G. Muckel

"Ask for help from your sponsor."—Elizabeth Sanger

"Have a true concern and genuine caring about your prospect."—Brian Soucier

"Be enthusiastic!"—Kiran Dulai

"Recruit while shopping."—Ann Wang

"Stay cheerful no matter what."—Michelle Mesecher

"Work with parents from sports and kids' activities." —Robbie Buchanan

"Focus, focus, focus."—Muriel Ferrari

"Spend time with people who are motivated and focused; learn everything you can and apply it."—Sheryl Mucker

"Be passionate and honest and give lots of support." —Terri Stroble

"You can't sell what you don't appear to be excited about yourself."—Patrice R. Jones

"Be open to learn from others, even the ones you are recruiting."—Mamie Mae Stone

"Believe in the company, in the product, and in yourself. You must believe!"—Rebecca L. Pence

"Ask your prospects, 'Do you want to make money or save money? Do you want your life to run you, or do you want to run your life?'"—Bernadette Ernissee

"I found that when recruiting, one thing that works well for me is the fact that I give people a choice. I talk to them about the 97 percent of people who retire broke. I talk about the advantages, which include time freedom, unlimited income opportunity, and the ability to be your own boss."
—Donna Elzey

"Use your 'affinity groups.' If you are a teacher, reach out to other educators. If you are in healthcare, reach out to others in your field. If you are the parents of twins, reach out to other parents of twins."—Dr. Emily A. Carey

"Always be truthful, and don't hesitate to let prospective partners know that to be successful requires work, time, and patience."—Gloria M. Baldwin

"Do recruiting with the kids in tow. People will see that real women can do this business."—Rebecca Saban

"If someone says no, move on! Do not 'defend' what you do to anyone. Believe in yourself and ignore the negatives."
—Lauré J. Riddle

"Learn to listen and ask positive questions that require a 'yes' answer."—Anita Bush

"The question is not whether to sponsor women into the network marketing industry, the substantial question is . . . who

and how many? The significant issue is to choose the most efficient and effective women in the marketplace and be able to utilize their strengths and talents.

"Choose young married women. Most are well-educated and goal-oriented. Today's young women are more prepared for business than their predecessors. These women are sharp; savvy; and they know what they want and more important, how to get it. Part of the sponsoring and training issues that this industry previously faced have disappeared with these young professionals as they bring their fresh skills to the workplace.

"Numerous young women have chosen to delay marriage. They graduate from a university with dreams and desire in hand, ready to take on the world. Career first and maybe family later. They are comfortable with being single. Young women are into relationships and partnerships. Twenty-first-century women are not taking a back seat to anyone, and they are not waiting for their prince to come either: They are creating their own kingdoms.

"Older women are treasures: Recruit all of them you can. They seem to have more time and energy and are better organized than most people. They not only have polished skills but also have incredible wisdom to offer. Their communications skills are exceptional, and their ability to manage, to be flexible, and to inspire others is a natural.

"Experience has proven that you cannot judge a book by its cover, and that goes for women, too. Large, small, short or tall, the most effective women are those who have a healthy self-esteem. Women of any age who have spent time on 'inner work' and have a sense of self are the ones you want on your team. They are usually rich in every area of their lives. A woman who is completely comfortable with herself is a

woman worth pure gold to any business that is fortunate enough to attract her." —*Pat Davis, President and Founder of Network Marketing Tutor, Inc.*

Women Helping Women

"The women in our organization support one another through a concept called 'Women on Fire' teams. We took the idea from an Upline *magazine article and ran with it. Our small teams of five to ten women (and we let men participate, too) communicate daily through our voicemail system. We set up weekly and daily goals and check in and out with each other. The purpose of the groups is to be accountable to someone (ultimately to yourself) and also to have encouragement and support during moments of triumph and moments of heartache (and those come too!). As a woman, I know that I need to 'talk through' everything, and most other woman do, too. These Women on Fire groups allow us the opportunity to talk about what's working and what's not. The unintended benefit is that these groups form a very strong bond ... they won't let the other ladies in their groups quit. We have seen a greatly higher retention rate among those (men, too) who participate in these teams."* —*Stephanie Stortz*

"We assign a mentor to new reps, and we have bonding sessions among the older ones. We also work in teams. This business is so much fun if you don't try to do it alone. We also do women's seminars and luncheons which address the challenges that females face." —*Betty Miles*

"The reason people stay with a company is the relationships they build. In order to help that team-building, I hold special

recognition luncheons, to thank my directors for a job well done on a quarterly basis. Lunch is on me, and a thank-you gift is given. This also gives the directors time to network on a social level. On a consultant level, I encourage 'batter bowl buddies.' Everyone puts their name in a batter bowl, you pick out a name and make the commitment to go see that person's presentation. By doing this it gives the consultant a helper during the show, and the helper gets to see the consultant's show style and learn new sales and recruiting techniques, thus fostering a relationship that can lead to networking together in the future."—Donna McDonald

Maintaining Balance in Your Life: What Others Do

WHILE SEVERAL WOMEN who talked to us indicated they have not yet successfully achieved balance, many others shared their methods for finding inner peace. Following is a collective recap of the most popular ways women told us they find balance in their lives. Consider which ones will work for you and add them to your daily routine.

- Take quiet time spiritually, physically, and emotionally each day
- Meditate
- Pray: talk and listen to God
- Keep a journal
- Exercise (bike, walk, swim, play tennis)
- Set goals and use a daily planner
- Read
- Go for a walk
- Make dates with your husband or significant other

- Treat scheduled times with your family and loved ones as if they were business appointments and stick to the schedule
- Go to movies, plays, and concerts
- Escape to a secluded area at least once a week just to relax
- Spend time with family and friends doing the things you love
- Listen to pleasant music as often as possible
- Connect with nature
- Walk the dog
- Do yoga
- Block negative people out of your life
- Spend forty-five minutes walking in nature. During that time, acknowledge individually all your blessings and thank God verbally for them.
- Keep a gratitude journal
- Play with dogs, do volunteer work, lift weights, sing
- Recognize each day as a gift. Decide today is going to be the best day yet.
- Block time for yourself and stick to it
- Paint and do crafts
- Stay focused on your dreams and put God first. He helps you balance when you listen to Him.
- Take about fifteen to twenty minutes per day to relax. Use aromatherapy and relaxation techniques.
- Involve your family in your dreams and goals and let them know they are valued as a priceless part of your life
- Put your family first. If you have a problem in your family life, it will affect your business.
- Attend church, sing in the choir, teach a Bible study class

- Hang out with young people and children. Learn again how to laugh and play.
- Seek guidance from seniors
- Laugh a lot and play with ferrets—they are too cute not to make you laugh!
- Learn to say no. When unreasonable demands are placed on your time, say no instead of becoming frustrated trying to fit something else into your already busy day.
- Don't sweat the small stuff
- Listen to music or read something light on the Stair Master
- Go to the park and play on the swing set
- Take care of yourself through proper nutrition

Choosing a Company

"Look for a company that is financially sound, has a management with integrity, good quality products, international markets, and a plan to provide distributors continuing opportunity by introducing new unrelated lines of product through divisionalization."—Marguerite Sung

"Look at the start-up costs. The company's reputation . . . Is it well-known? Check out their background with the Better Business Bureau. Is the product you will be selling a renewable product? Is it a product you truly believe in?"
—Miki Crowl

"Anyone looking for a network marketing business should make sure the company:

- *Is at least eighteen months old*
- *Is at the beginning of its global expansion*
- *Has a consumable or disposable product that they guarantee*
- *Is a company you can be proud of*
- *Offers a fair playing field so that those who come into the business a few years down the line have just as much chance to be successful as the original participants*
- *Stays on the cutting edge*

"I prefer a publicly traded company"—Susan Elizabeth Waitley

"Women today should look for products and a corporate philosophy that they relate to. Most people, especially women, must fall in love with the products first. Also, they need to experience the culture of the company and trust their intuition about what they see."—Robin B. Cohen

What It Takes

"Women have the power to build successful businesses and have financial freedom, but [success] does not come overnight. It requires time and hard work."—Miki Crowl

"[Some] people think they can just join a network marketing business and make lots of money without much time and effort. Then when it fails (surprise!) they blame the network marketing industry. This is a business just like any other, which will require hard work and persistence. If [people] are willing to pay the price, they will reap the rewards!"—Lili Willick

"You need to be a bit of a risk taker to do well. What works best, I believe, in this business is making the effort. We have no control over results, only efforts. I also think that concentrating on approaching people the way you would want to be approached is important. I think salespeople would be a lot better off to get rid of their 'spiels' and be themselves."
—Kerry Lynn Buskirk

"Being self-disciplined [is what it takes]. At first I was not [disciplined], and the business consumed me 24/7. This did not work, and the last few years I took Sundays completely off, also no calls during dinner. I pick my daughter up from school every day and have time with her. That way, if I have a meeting at night, it's okay. I have developed a whole training [program] around teaching others to develop a presidential habit—specific call time that they are committed to daily so that there is no guilt! When you are with your kids, you do not want to be thinking, 'I should be making calls!' And when you are making calls, you don't want to be thinking, 'I should be with my kids!' This will kill you with guilt. A disciplined daily action will save you!"
—Grace Dulaney

General Business Tips

"I encourage everyone to write a vision statement and to update it regularly. The vision statement is a reminder [to people] of why they're doing their business. I also encourage affirmations and visualization and really monitoring self-talk. I send them monthly audio tapes, 'A Message from Margaret,' as a way to keep my voice in their ears on a monthly basis."—Margaret Tanaka

"Find out how to manage your taxes early on in your business. Multilevel marketing is fantastic for tax breaks and benefits."—Revae Stuart

"Listen to books on tape to maximize driving time." —Renee Scudder

"Always give good customer care."—Sue Marteeny

Appendix 2: Resources _____

M OST OF THE RESOURCES listed below are readily available at bookstores, on newsstands, or on the Web. For harder-to-find items, we have included ordering information.

Books

NETWORK MARKETING

> *Your First Year in Network Marketing* by Mark Yarnell and Rene Reid Yarnell
>
> *Mary Kay on People Management* by Mary Kay Ash
>
> *Being the Best You Can Be in MLM,* and, *17 Secrets of Master Prospectors* by John Kalench
>
> *Come to the Table: A Celebration of Family Life* by Doris Christopher
>
> *Building a Successful Network Marketing Company* by Angela L. Moore
>
> *The American Dream* by Betty Miles (800-493-9334)
>
> *The Miracle of Intention: A Handbook for Defining Your Success* by Pat Davis (888-952-7000)

Heart to Heart: The Real Power of Network Marketing by Scott DeGarmo and Louis Tartaglia, M.D.

The Inner World of Network Marketing by Carole Munson and Dondi Robbins

Wave 4: Network Marketing in the 21st Century by Richard Poe

The Greatest Networker in the World and *Conversations with the Greatest Networker in the World: More of the Story* by J. Milton Fogg

PERSONAL GROWTH/INSPIRATION

Women of Courage: Inspiring Stories from the Women Who Lived Them by Katherine Martin

Take Time for Your Life: A Personal Coach's 7-Step Program for Creating the Life You Want by Cheryl Richardson

The Game of Life and How to Play It by Florence Scovel-Shinn

The Seat of the Soul by Gary Zukav

The Seven Spiritual Laws of Success by Deepak Chopra

Feel the Fear and Do It Anyway by Susan Jeffers

The Power of Your Subconscious Mind by Joseph Murphy

Life Strategies by Phillip C. McGraw, Ph.D.

Reinventing the Individual: You! by Bud Markos (800-799-9171)

The 21 Most Powerful Minutes in a Leader's Day and *The 21 Indispensable Qualities of a Leader* by John Maxwell

Dream Big by Cynthia Stewart-Copier

Dare to Dream and Work to Win by Dr. Tom Barrett

Don't Sweat the Small Stuff —and It's All Small Stuff, by Richard Carlson

Unstoppable: 45 Powerful Stories of Perseverance and Triumph from People Just Like You by Cynthia Kersey

SALES/MARKETING

How to Become a Rainmaker: The Rules for Getting and Keeping Customers and Clients by Jeffrey J. Fox

Selling the Invisible: A Field Guide to Modern Marketing by Harry Beckwith

EVEolution: The Eight Truths of Marketing to Women by Faith Popcorn and Lys Marigold

FINANCES

Multiple Streams of Income: How to Generate a Lifetime of Unlimited Wealth by Robert G. Allen

The Courage to Be Rich: Creating a Life of Material and Spiritual Abundance by Suze Orman

Your Money or Your Life: Transforming Your Relationship with Money and Achieving Financial Independence by Joe Dominguez and Vicki Robin

Smart Women Finish Rich: 7 Steps to Achieving Financial Security and Funding Your Dreams by David Bach

Rich Dad, Poor Dad and *Cashflow Quadrant* by Robert T. Kiyosaki

The Millionairess Across the Street by Jennifer Bayse Sander and Bettina R. Flores

Think and Grow Rich by Napoleon Hill

Magazines

Upline (www.upline.com or 877-898-8882)

Network Marketing Lifestyles (www.nmlifestyles.com or 877-898-8882)

Success Magazine (www.successmagazine.com or 919-807-1100)

O: The Oprah Magazine (www.oprah.com)

Working Women Magazine

Audio Tapes

The Women's Tapes: Conversations with Six Masters of Network Marketing

A Message from Margaret (www.hightideproductions.net; 619-615-9895)

What to Look for and What to Look Out for in Multilevel Marketing by Kevin Grimes (Sound Concepts: 800-723-8446)

Web Sites

All are preceded by www.

dsa.org (a listing of member companies with information about them)

networkmarketingtutor.com (a training tips newsletter)

Whoohoo.net (daily motivation and fun)

bluemountain.com (free e-cards)

Appendix 3: Acknowledgments _____

T HE JOY OF WRITING this book came from our connections to so many wonderful individuals. All were willing to share of themselves to help women understand what network marketing and direct selling can offer to enhance their lives. We would like to gratefully acknowledge all the women, and the men, who graciously worked with us to make this book a reality. Since there were so many people involved, if we have inadvertently left anyone out, we sincerely apologize for the oversight. We appreciate everyone's contribution!

Independent women business owners who completed questionnaires or were interviewed about their stories:

Valerie Bagnol, Mary Kay Inc.
Kerry Lynn Buskirk, Mary Kay Inc.
Diane Chapman, Excel Communications, Inc.
Robin B. Cohen, Oxyfresh Worldwide, Inc.
Miki Crowl, Avon Products, Inc.
Cheryl Dockery, Primerica

Grace Dulaney, Big Planet
Tami Fingerle, Weekenders USA, Inc.
Diane Grunseich, Excel Communications, Inc.
Karen Hagen, Watkins, Inc.
Suzie Kaster, Oxyfresh Worldwide, Inc.
Molly Maxey, Excel Communications, Inc.
Nancy Wright Maxwell, The Southwestern Co.
Donna McDonald, The Pampered Chef
Betty Miles, Excel Communications, Inc.
Therese Razzante, The Longaberger Company
Nancy Jo Ryan, The Pampered Chef
Stephanie R. Stortz, Excel Communications, Inc.
Marguerite Sung, Nu Skin USA
Margaret Tanaka, Shaklee Corporation
Carol Totten, Excel Communications, Inc.
Susan Elizabeth Waitley, USANA Health Sciences
Carolyn A. Ward, Mary Kay Inc.
Michelle Watts, Oxyfresh Worldwide, Inc.
Lili Willick, Watkins, Inc.

Individuals who helped direct us to stories or provided input, expertise or support:

Carolyn Aishton, Avon Products, Inc.
Delores Antune, Watkins, Inc.
Anita Bush, TARRAH Cosmetics
Dianne Beck, The Pampered Chef
Victor Beaudet, Avon Products, Inc.
Nancy Brenner, Shaklee Corporation
Richard Brooke, Oxyfresh Worldwide, Inc.

Laura Brown, House of Lloyd
Don Carne, Incomnet
Laura Castellano, Avon Products, Inc.
Lea Clark, Tupperware Corporation
Doug Cloward, Cloward and Associates
Pat Davis, Network Marketing Tutor, Inc.
Christina Dettler, Home Culinarian
Jane Edwards, The Pampered Chef
Heidi Everett, The Antioch Corporation
Marjorie Fine, Shaklee Corporation
Beth FitzGibbon, FitzGibbon & Associates
Cheryl Flood, Weekenders USA, Inc.
Sue Frederickson, Excel Communications, Inc.
Susan Gessner, Avon Products, Inc.
Diana Gold, Mary Kay Inc.
Kevin Grimes, Grimes & Reese
Pat Hintze, Excel Field Leader
Carol Hukari, Shaklee Corporation
Candace Keefe, Arbonne International
Dallin Larsen, USANA Health Sciences
Versa Lauritsen, Avon Products, Inc.
Karyn Leniek, The Pampered Chef
Debbie Linchesky, The Pampered Chef
Christine Male, The Longaberger Company
D'Arcy McKay, McKay Consulting
Tori Mathe, Excel Communications, Inc.
Russell R. Mack, Mary Kay Inc.
Krista McKinney, The Pampered Chef
Julianna Much, Weekenders USA, Inc.
Tish Poling, Intimate Brands
Spencer Reese, Grimes & Reese
Kay Richter, The Antioch Corporation

Justin Rose, Big Planet
Alice Siesto, Tupperware Corporation
Bob Sircy, The Southwestern Company
Bill Spears, Tupperware Corporation
Marla Stinbellenberg, Creative Memories
Shannon Summers, Mary Kay Inc.
Jerry Taylor, Direct Selling Education Foundation
Mary Walls, Excel Communications, Inc.
Anna Watson, The Pampered Chef
Tom Whatley, Mary Kay Inc.
Connie White, Mary Kay Inc.
Jann Woods, Grimes & Reese
Madeline Zeisner, Mary Kay Inc.

Corporate executive contributors of personal stories or quotes:

Leslie Campbell, TARRAH Cosmetics
Doris Christopher, The Pampered Chef
Marielena Cirolia, Your Gentle Spirit, Inc
Charlene Knox, Nu Skin USA
Cheryl Lightle, Creative Memories
Russell Mack, Mary Kay Inc.
Rosemary Redmond, Weekenders
Jill Sands, JS HomeStyle
Rene Stutz, Home Culinarian

Tips and Resources Contributors

THESE ARE INDEPENDENT network marketing representatives who attended a Women's Perspective Seminar in September 2000 and provided input for the book via questionnaires completed at that event:

Erin Anderson

Carol Arp

Gloria M. Baldwin

Jan Beaty

Marie A. Brooks

Robbie Buchanan

Anita Bush

Andrea Canaday

Dr. Emily A. Carey

Dianne Carter

Deborah Coronado

Bertha Couch

Tammy L. Cowden

Katharine Crusius

Pat Curington

Vera L. Curry

Louisa Curtis

Catherine K. Davis

Lorry Davis

JoAnne Diaz

Takila Douglas

Joyce Duggan

Kiran Dulai

Donna Elzey

Bernadette Ernissee

Cheryl E. Feiling

Muriel Ferrari

Regina Fisher

Michelle Gent

Linda Goodman

Lucretia Goodson

Lisa Groff

Barbara Hails

Elaine Hankins

Nancy Harris

Peggy Himes

Kerri Hodges

Frances Jeffers

Patrice R. Jones

Pamela Jurkovac

Krissy Jutte

Monika S. Kennemur

Roxanna M. Kirby

Sharon Kramer

Karen Lamberson

Elizabeth Lewis

Teresita Licuanan

Cindy Malar

Sue Marteeny

Michele May

Michelle Mesecher

Marie C. Miller

Heide Morris

Patty Morris

Jill Mowell

Barbara G. Muckel

Sheryl Mucker

Lorraine Munoz

Marianna Panetta
Lois Parrish
Rebecca L. Pence
Cathie Pierce
Diane Priest
Heide Rauenzahn
Kathleen Rayhawk
Llewellyn J. Rhoe
Lauré J. Riddle
Nancy Ross
Rebecca Saban
Elizabeth Sanger
Jennifer Schmidt
Renee Scudder
Pat Baird Sessler

Lola Shearer
Lori Sherman
Suzanne Short
Brian Soucier
Mamie Mae Stone
Shelly Stratton
Terri Stroble
Revae Stuart
Rebecca Thomas
Ann Wang
Ellen Weber
Helen Wells
Jeanne L. Wendt
Crystal Wilkerson
Angela A. Woppman

Prima Publishing support staff:

Michelle McCormack, project editor
Susan Silva, acquisitions editor
David Richardson, acquisitions editor
Matt Jarrette, publicist

Our sincere gratitude and warm best wishes to all these wonderful friends!

Index